PACK UP YOUR TROUBLES

D1615318

TO RECRUITING OFFICE

YOU[R]
COUN[TRY]
NEEDS
YOU

"FALL IN, AND FOLLOW ME!"

Conway
An imprint of Bloomsbury Publishing Plc

50 Bedford Square   1385 Broadway
London   New York
WC1B 3DP   NY 10018
UK   USA

www.bloomsbury.com

CONWAY and the 'C' logo are trademarks of Bloomsbury Publishing Plc
First published 2016

© James Taylor, 2016

James Taylor has asserted his right under the Copyright, Designs and
Patents Act, 1988, to be identified as Author of this work.

All rights reserved. No part of this publication may be reproduced or
transmitted in any form or by any means, electronic or mechanical,
including photocopying, recording, or any information storage or
retrieval system, without prior permission in writing from the publishers.

No responsibility for loss caused to any individual or organization acting
on or refraining from action as a result of the material in this publication
can be accepted by Bloomsbury or the author.

British Library Cataloguing-in-Publication Data
A catalogue record for this book is available from the British Library.

Library of Congress Cataloguing-in-Publication data has been applied for.

ISBN: PB: 978-1-8448-6341-9
ePDF: 978-1-8448-6343-3
ePub: 978-1-8448-6342-6

2 4 6 8 10 9 7 5 3 1

Typeset in 8.75/12.5 ITC Cheltenham by Carrdesignstudio.com
Printed and bound in China by RRD Asia Printing Solutions Limited

This book is dedicated to James Brazier
for sharing his enthusiasm and knowledge
of Great War comic postcards.

WE ALL LOVE JACK.

Bloomsbury Publishing Plc makes every effort to ensure that the
papers used in the manufacture of our books are natural, recyclable
products made from wood grown in well-managed forests. Our
manufacturing processes conform to the environmental regulations of
the country of origin.

To find out more about our authors and books visit www.bloomsbury.
com. Here you will find extracts, author interviews, details of
forthcoming events and the option to sign up for our newsletters.

BOTH DRESSED TO KILL

PACK UP YOUR TROUBLES

How Humorous Postcards Helped to Win World War I

JAMES TAYLOR

KHAKI

THIS STUFF WILL NEVER SHRINK!

C
CONWAY
BLOOMSBURY
LONDON · OXFORD · NEW YORK · NEW DELHI · SYDNEY

CONTENTS

ACKNOWLEDGEMENTS

Many people have been generous with their expertise and knowledge. I would especially like to thank the staff of the British Library; the Cartoon Museum, London; the Imperial War Museum; the National Maritime Museum, Greenwich; the National Archives; the Victoria & Albert Museum; and Tristan Pollard, Curatorial and Technical Manager, Royal West of England Academy.

I would also like to thank fellow postcard enthusiasts and collectors for their advice, expertise and in some instances assistance with illustrations, namely Tony Allen; Bernard Barrett; Dr Nick Hiley; Brian Lund; Roger Mayhew; and David Marks who kindly contributed the chapter on the 'War in the Air'. Bernard Crossley kindly read through the draft manuscript and made several helpful suggestions with regard to Donald McGill and Reg Maurice.

Thanks also goes to James Bissell-Thomas, the owner of the Donald McGill Museum in Ryde, Isle of Wight; Ian Wallace, the copyright holder of Bamforth & Co postcards and Webster Wickham, grandson of Mabel Lucie Attwell. Also, Mark and Sally Wingham, the publishers of *Picture Postcard Monthly*, and Josh Taylor for his administrative support.

Gratitude to James Brazier for his advice, encouragement and support from start to finish. He has been a guiding light and generously supplied many of the cards. Finally the team at Bloomsbury including Janet Murphy and my editor Jenny Clark for believing in this project and bringing it to fruition.

"After You, Mother!"

Home-on-leave Tommy's enthusiasm for the fairer sex is highlighted in this cheeky card by Lawson Wood, published by Inter-Art Co.

INTRODUCTION

Pack Up Your Troubles tells the story of how the artist-drawn humorous postcard in Britain helped to win World War I (1914–1918) or, as it is also known, the Great War. It outlines the origins, development and popularity of the genre from the 1840s to 1918; examines the achievements, backgrounds and personalities of the main protagonists and their professional and social networks across the text and in dedicated biographical entries; looks at the range of their artistic styles, comic techniques and subjects, employed not only to amuse and entertain but also to convey government-approved instructions, messages

SOMETHING ATTEMPTED---SOMETHING DONE.

A youthful parody of German destruction wrought against Britain and her allies. Harold Earnshaw, published by Valentine and Sons.

and propaganda to a mass audience; addresses the essential roles of the General Post Office and the Army Postal Service in the sorting, censorship, distribution and delivery of mail; and also examines the crucial work of Wellington House in London, the headquarters of British wartime propaganda. In addition, the book highlights the role of the artists' agents and the wide range of postcard publishers. Finally, some of the messages written on the postcards are featured especially if they reveal the reason why the senders selected the specific cards.

The Khaki Boy: "If I had known that tunnel was so long, I'd have kissed you."
The Mauve Girl: "Gracious! didn't you? Somebody did"!

Are we downhearted?

No!!!

Bombadear
Tottie
of the
5th Flappers.

THE HUMOROUS POSTCARD IN WORLD WAR I

The number of professional artists closely associated with the design of humorous postcards (or 'comic cards', as collectors call them) about Great War subjects was upwards of 50, of which about 35 were selected for this book. The criteria applied to the selection were: that the artists worked in Britain, or served in the British Army; they were passionate about the genre and produced significant numbers of consistently high-quality colour designs; or, if they created fewer cards, that these were extraordinary in terms of artistic technique, subject and style. They might be ingeniously absurd, 'cutesy' (the first known use

"WHAT'S THAT MAN BITIN' THAT POOR LADY FOR ?"

of this word dates from 1914), quirky, or even offer something else – that special X-factor that singles them out from what was then a very competitive and overcrowded visual-joke market.

The label 'postcard artists' is used here for convenience, although it is a little misleading; almost all of them had to turn their hand to other art forms to make ends meet, such as advertising, cartooning, and book- and magazine-illustration. Donald McGill holds the record for focusing exclusively on this genre across six decades.

Fig 1 Tommy canoodling with a young lady is seen in a very different light by two observing dogs. Donald McGill, published by Inter-Art Co.

The principal men who produced postcard designs during the war years, in alphabetical order, include:

Bruce Bairnsfather	Fergus Mackain
Arthur Butcher	FE Morgan
Dudley Buxton	Ernest Noble
Reg Carter	Geo Piper
AR Cattley	Sid A Potts
Geo Davey	GE Shepheard
Harold Earnshaw	Fred Spurgin
Archibald English	GA Stevens
T Gilson	W Stocker Shaw
Fred Gothard	GE Studdy
Alfred Leete	Doug Tempest
FG Lewin	Bert Thomas
Reg Maurice	Louis Wain
Donald McGill	Lawson Wood

Of the small group of women, the following were standout artists:

Mabel Lucie Attwell	AA Nash
Nina K Brisley	Agnes Richardson
HGC Marsh-Lambert	Flora White

Many of the cards of Adrienne A Nash and Helen GC Marsh-Lambert were patriotic and sentimental and the subjects depicted mean that they wouldn't be considered as mainstream comic cards by modern collectors. The same applies to the glamorous designs of alluring wartime ladies by Arthur Butcher, although a high proportion of these artists' cards raise a smile and for that reason a few of them are featured here. One such card depicts a close-up view of a young lady's lips and is captioned with the double entendre, 'Come On Now And Do Your Bit!' (See Fig 2b).

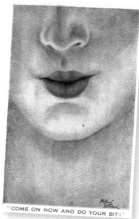

Fig 2a This card was sent by the girlfriend of Private William Soane on 19 October 1916 who was serving in Northern France. A week later he died of his wounds sustained on the Somme.

Fig 2b A quirky close-up view of a lady's lipsticked lips. Both cards by Arthur Butcher, published by Inter-Art Co.

Some artists only used their initials, pseudonym or a single name. They include:

AE (Archibald English), who, among other things, created designs of conscientious objectors;

Chalker, who parodied recruitment;

GAS (GA Stevens), who, together with GE Shepheard (who also used initials, GES), designed quirky comic silhouettes of camp life and training for Photochrom Co;

Glanville, who produced lively scenes of army life for Millar & Lang Art Publishing Co;

FG (Fred Gothard), who had a predilection for ginger-haired comic characters;

PHLO (artist not yet known), who made some striking cards of Royal Flying Corps subjects; and **VWS** (VW Sternberg), whose subjects and style are reminiscent of some of the work of the women artists.

Compared to the extensive database of information about British painters and printmakers, many biographies of these postcard artists remain at best sketchy. Ten of the artists – Mabel Lucie Attwell, Bruce Bairnsfather, Harold Earnshaw, Alfred Leete, Fergus Mackain, Donald McGill, Fred Spurgin, Doug Tempest, Bert Thomas and Lawson Wood – are featured in greater detail below to draw out the key aspects of their remarkable and wide-ranging contribution to the genre.

Brief history of the artist-drawn comic postcard

The world's earliest-recorded picture postcard was sold at auction in March 2002 for the sum of £31,750 (including commission). Stamped with a Penny Black, it was sent in 1840 to Theodore Edward Hook (1788–1844), who lived in Fulham, London some three years after Queen Victoria came to the throne. Hook was a composer, civil servant (briefly), playboy, playwright, prankster, man of letters and novelist, noted at the time for his wit and drollery. It is likely that he created the card for his own amusement and sent it to himself as a joke. It's an artist-drawn hand-coloured humorous card that pokes fun at the postal service by depicting the Post Office scribes seated around a vast inkwell on which is written the word 'Official'. In comparison with the caustic work of the British caricaturist James Gillray, however, it is mild-mannered.

In 1894, a change to official British postal regulations led to the practice of sending picture postcards being actively encouraged. From 1899, the standard size of 5½in x 3½in for a postcard was introduced, which brought Britain in line with other countries. By 1902, the 'divided back' enabled people to write messages on one half of the back of the card with the other dedicated to the address, thereby leaving the front free for a picture. During the Edwardian era many more artists, both amateur and professional, had their original art designs – created in pencil, or pen-and-ink with watercolour – scaled down and printed for private or public circulation. Photography was adopted early on in the history of the picture postcard but is outside of the sphere of interest of this publication. That said, some postcard artists and publishers adapted and copied photographs to produce comic work.

Bamforth & Co, in Holmfirth, West Yorkshire was one of the most successful pioneering companies, which initially created lantern slides then moved into the production of silent films (intermittently from 1898 to 1918), and also produced postcards of humorous, patriotic and sentimental subjects. It had been established by James Bamforth in 1870 and by the early 1900s the company emerged as a leading player in the design of comic cards that poked fun at every aspect of human nature, with a very strong suit in seaside cards that in later decades became increasingly saucy and vulgar. In 1905, the company had branches in London and New York. By the end of the war, it had grown to become the world's largest producer of comic cards, with around 20 million printed annually. The outstanding long-term employee was Doug Tempest, who by 1910 worked there as a staff artist. He produced cards covering many wartime subjects, including anti-Kaiser comic cards, although he, like McGill, is best remembered for his provocative seaside postcards.

Norfolk-born Tempest (1887–1954) was the son of a school-master. He studied at Leeds School of Art, where he won several prizes. Unable to join the army due to a heart defect, Tempest was able to contribute to the war effort through his artistic talent and ability to make people laugh. As Tony Allen, the Great War-postcard collector, author and blogger observed, the artist's 'wartime comic illustrations capitalised on the British ability to laugh at themselves in times of hardship and he produced cards to encourage recruitment, made jokes about food shortages, made fun of munitions work and poked gentle fun at convalescent soldiers'.

From the outset, one of the most popular subject categories of the picture postcard was humour. An explanation as to why the postcard in general was so popular in the 1910s is summarised by the economic and social historian David M Williams, formerly of the University of Leicester, in *A New Medium for Advertising: The Postcard, 1900–1920* (1988). Williams observes that 'the postcard was attractive in three ways: as a useful and cheap means of communication, as a memento or souvenir, and as an interesting and often colourful item in its own right'.

Williams went on to say that 'in an age when telephones were few and personalised transport limited, the postcard was the ideal form of communication and had the virtue of being simpler and less demanding than the formal letter. Brevity was the essence of the postcard message. The attraction of the medium to a newly literate and more mobile population was enormous.'

Postcards were a popular source of interest, fascination and fun as there was a subject to suit pretty much every taste, occasion and sentiment. They were also widely available and affordable, with thousands of cards on sale on every high street across the country. The online site www.worldwar1postcards.com highlights their visibility and the ease with which buyers could access them during the war on both the Home and Western Fronts: 'The newsagents WHSmith displayed numerous categories of war-related cards in their postal racks of its 2,000 shops. In addition, booksellers, cinemas, corner shops, stationery stores, public houses, haberdashery stores, post offices and branches of Boots the Chemist and numerous other commercial outlets sold them. By 1915, "war cards" were also displayed and offered in thousands of YMCA canteens in military training camps at home and on the Western Front and elsewhere.'

Card prices ranged from a halfpenny to a penny or less if they were bought in bulk. Until 3 June 1918, the price of a stamp was a halfpenny inland and one penny worldwide. From 1 September 1914, the postage was free for those serving in the armed forces on the continent as long as the item did not exceed 4oz in weight. Postcards were avidly collected across all classes and were stored in albums to be shown to family and friends. The speed and frequency of mail delivery was also impressive given the technology then available; it was normal for there to be multiple deliveries a day to some postal areas on the Home Front, making the exchange of picture postcards a precursor to the interactions now enabled by Facebook, Flickr, Tumblr, Twitter and e-mail, albeit in an elementary form.

The language of stamps

Comic artists also designed Great War postcards that offered a visual explanation of the 'Language of Stamps'. William Cochrane addressed this zany subject in *The Philatelic Database* (1 May 2013). Stamps were affixed to envelopes and picture postcards in all sorts of odd positions and angles, which conveyed a message to the recipient. This custom had developed in England during the 19th century and soon spread to other countries, although several different systems were in use. One postcard, published by Inter-Art Co as part of its 'Comique' series and titled 'The Language of Stamps', features stamps placed in various positions to denote the following: Write soon; A kiss; I love you; Do you remember me?; With all my Heart; Thinking of you; Answer at once; and Do you love me? (See Fig 3 overleaf).

Many other such explanatory comic cards were published by Inter-Art Co and the Regent Publishing Co during the period, although the artist's name is not usually given. After the war, however, postal administrators clamped down on this practice, forcing the sender to place stamps in the right-hand corner of the card or envelope in an upright position.

Fig 3 'The Language of Stamps'. Artist unknown, published by Inter-Art Co.

Postcard publications

The popularity of postcards led to the publication of specialist journals and magazines. Two published in London were *The Postcard. The smallest monthly journal, etc.* and *The Postcard Connoisseur: a monthly magazine of announcement and criticism for post-card collectors. With descriptions & specimens.* Copies are now extremely hard to find, although the British Library holds numbers 1 to 4 of the former from 1893, and numbers 1 to 3 of the latter for the year 1904. The latter, priced at 6p, was small both in format and number of pages. In its first issue, launched in March 1904, the editorial explained that the publication

had been established because of the postcard's popularity and that: 'it will depend for its main support on those who realise what a powerful aid the post-card pictorial can be to art, knowledge, and good feeling.'

The British Library also has (or in fact *had*) a series of *The Postcard: A magazine of travel, philately, art, etc.* that ran from July 1900 (Vol 1) to September 1907 (Vol 8), although the magazines are now officially listed on their website as 'mislaid'.

The postcard goes to war

The postcards used in the war fall into three main categories: the official Field Service postcards; commercial picture cards; and the embroidered silk cards that were offered at higher prices and sent as keepsakes. The comic cards belong mainly in the second category. Martha Hanna in *Letters: Communication between Front and Home Front* (2014) states that the Field Service postcards (FSPCs) were 'roundly despised as impersonal and almost completely uninformative. They offered a pre-printed menu of options – from "I am quite well" to "I am being sent down to the base" – British soldiers had to heed the emphatic warning that "If anything else is added to the post card it will be destroyed."'

According to the postal historian Alistair Kennedy, the upside of the FSPCs was that they were 'a convenient way

Fig 4 The dull tick-box official Field Service postcard was a gift-horse to the comic artists. Artist unknown, published by Art Publishers (Accrington) Ltd, Manchester.

for soldiers to assure their families that they were alive and well when there was no time to write a letter.'

Anthony Richards in *The Telegraph* (30 May 2014) recounted one notable exception to Hanna's opinion, observing that 'Captain Billie Nevill, who later found fame for kicking a football ahead of the advance on the first day of the Battle of the Somme [1 July 1916], confirmed the importance of such postcards: "It's a wonderful thing, a Field Service postcard. It costs nothing, takes no time, and gives no mental energy. It is in fact the essence of laziness, the ideal of the wordless correspondent and the bored nephew alike. From it may spring a parcel, a letter, anything!"'

Hanna's viewpoint on the whole, however, is correct. The FSPCs were not widely liked and were parodied by postcard artists (see Fig 4). One example by Donald McGill, published by Inter-Art Co, depicts a small, cute dog with

"Only a measly Field Postcard again. I believe he's keeping another dog ! "
"Encore une simple carte postale ! Je crois qu'il me trompe !"

downcast eyes and its paws resting on a FSPC. It is captioned: 'Only a measly Field Postcard again. I believe he's keeping another dog!' (See Fig 5). FSPCs were also parodied by serving soldiers on the Western Front. A feature headlined 'Humorous Suggestions From The Front' published in the *Liverpool Echo* (11 November 1915) reveals the ingenuity of the Tommies from the Gloucester Territorials in suggesting replacement lines for dull official text. One offered the soldier the option of stating that he was: 'up to … my … eyes … in mud.'

The General Post Office and Royal Engineers (Postal Division)

Today, the importance of the British Post Office in the war is often overlooked. Strictly speaking, the service was called the General Post Office (GPO), and it was founded by King Charles II in 1660. More than 300 years later, in 1969, the assets of

Fig 5 Cute animals in various guises were a very popular Great War comic subject. Donald McGill, published by Inter-Art Co.

that business were transferred to The Post Office and it later developed into a sophisticated state postal system and telecommunications' carrier. In 1914, according to The Postal Museum's online records, the GPO employed more than 250,000 people. They indicate that the business generated an annual revenue of £32 million, which made it 'the biggest economic enterprise in Britain and the largest single employer in the world.' Also that on the eve of war, 'the GPO not only handled a yearly total of 5.9 billion items of post but was responsible for the nation's telegraph and telephone systems, as well as providing savings bank and other municipal facilities at thousands of branch offices'.

Kennedy notes in his 'Postal history from British forces on the Western Front in 1914' (*Stamp Magazine*, August 2014) that 'a postal service for British forces in France and Belgium was provided by the Royal Engineers (Postal Division) and a small Army Post Office (APO) was based at each formation headquarters from brigade level upwards, and further offices at divisional supply bases and railheads. In addition there were post offices at suitable places on the lines of communication, and larger ones at bases.'

Members of the Royal Engineers (Postal Division) were predominately recruited from the GPO. They worked in tandem to ensure that all mail was delivered from Britain to the service men and women abroad. In order to do this, the GPO's Home Depot constructed a massive wooden structure covering 5 acres of Regent's Park in London, where the post was sorted prior to despatch. It was believed to have been the largest structure of its kind in the world and by 1918 more than 2,500 staff, predominately female, worked there. From May 1917, members of the Women's Army Auxiliary Corps (WAAC) recruited from the GPO were employed at the Base Army Post Offices (BAPO) and the stationary Army Post Offices (APO) located on the Western Front.

The speed of delivery of mail from Britain to the British Expeditionary Force (BEF) was greatly improved when packet boats, the vessels that transported the mail, were introduced between Folkestone and Boulogne-sur-Mer, where an extensive BAPO had been established in January 1915. The transit time for mail was subsequently reduced from four to two days. It remained active until March 1919.

During the war, the Home Depot handled a whopping 114 million parcels and 2 billion letters. The number of postcards was included in the number of letters and of these the comic artist-drawn cards counted for a significant proportion, running into millions. In addition, there were millions of cards that were also acquired not for posting but to be added to a personal collection, for exchange or to be given as a gift in person.

Receiving post was one of the highlights of the arduous day-to-day life of the soldiers on the Western Front. Tony Allen recollects Private Frederick E Noakes's passionate opinion about the importance of receiving a parcel, postcard or letter on the Western Front. He wrote, 'Out here news of home is like food and drink to us, however trivial. Indeed, this life is like a dream and the old life the only reality. We live on memories.'

Post was also delivered to sailors, who collected their mail from designated ports, and the airmen who were initially attached to air-wings of the Army and Royal Navy. They merged together later in the war, on 1 April 1918, to form the Royal Air Force (RAF).

The censorship of post destined for Blighty (the slang word soldiers used for Britain and also for a non-life-threatening wound that would ensure a soldier was returned home) took place close to where the men served on the Western Front. The act of censorship, under the watchful eyes of unit officers, was necessary to stop vital information useful to the enemy being accidentally or deliberately given away, and also to prevent the spread of bad news that could lower morale and resilience. The commercial postcards and other missives were stamped by a numbered censor's hand-stamp issued to each unit.

The act of censorship itself also attracted the interest of many of the postcard artists. These included the gifted and prolific Fred Spurgin who is rated second only in popularity to Donald McGill among many card collectors today. Born Izydor Spungin (1885–1966) and of Russian origin, Spurgin

changed his name after arriving in Britain with his family in about 1899. According to an article in the April 1986 issue of *Picture Postcard Monthly* (*PPM*) by Brian Lund, the former publisher of said magazine, the family initially settled in Birmingham where his father developed a successful furniture business. As is evidenced by the fact that cards from as early as 1902 have been found, Spurgin preferred to focus his attention on drawing rather than furniture. Lund also notes that he used initials and a pseudonym early on in his career, probably because he was concerned that a Jewish name might be detrimental to sales.

The Great War postcard-and-ephemera collector James Brazier also uncovered new details about the artist, in part through an examination of the 1911 census. This led to a revision of the artist's birth and death dates. Brazier notes that in this case the census return is particularly valuable as 'Fred Spurgin completed it and his signature is identical to that sometimes shown on his postcard designs.' By that time the whole family was living in Brixton, London, where Spurgin's father was repairing watches and jewellery and Fred was working as an 'artist and designer'.

Some of Spurgin's early cards were published by W & AK Johnston and by Gale & Polden in the 1902–1904 period, and he later worked for many others, including J Beagles & Co, Inter-Art Co and the Regent Publishing Co. Lund describes him as 'The versatile Fred Spurgin' and believes that he holds the record for producing comic postcards for the greatest number of publishers. By 1915, Maurice, one of Spurgin's brothers, had established the Art and Humour Publishing Co as an outlet for Fred's comic cards.

In addition to all of these cards Spurgin, unlike McGill, was also a prolific book-illustrator and enjoyed commercial success during his lifetime, a fact that is confirmed by his prestigious marriage after the war to Lily Rothman, a daughter of the family then renowned for manufacturing Rothmans cigarettes.

Spurgin remained active throughout the Great War, the last part of which coincided with the end of the 'Golden Age' of postcards, the demise of which came about gradually and then markedly after 3 June 1918, when the British Treasury – desperate to raise extra revenue – increased inland postal rates from a halfpenny to a penny for postcards.

Postcard humour: origins, development and types

The artistic humour represented on wartime postcards originated in part from a long-standing British literary tradition that can be traced back to the comedic and censorious episodes in Chaucer's *The Canterbury Tales*, which was first published in print in 1476. These tales feature fictional characters that reveal the customs and practices of medieval England and are critical – especially of the Church – ironic, entertaining and open to interpretation.

That said, by far the most dominant force in the development of British humour was the 19th-century phenomenon of the British music hall: a mixture of comedy, music and songs, speciality acts and variety entertainment that was immensely popular from about the 1850s until the 1960s. The bawdy and the cheeky, catchphrases, double-entendres, innuendo, sarcasm and wit were all actively encouraged by the music hall and struck a popular chord across all classes in Britain – although this was not always readily admitted by the upper echelons of society – and these characteristics crossed over to the artist-drawn comic postcard.

The British passion for popular songs found its way on to the front of wartime postcards. Composers and lyricists adapted music and songs created before the war for military purposes, especially for marching and they also produced material during the war for the Army and the Royal Navy.

Two of the most celebrated and enduring ones adopted by the army as marching songs remain favourites today: 'It's a Long Way to Tipperary' and 'Pack Up Your Troubles in Your Old Kit-Bag, and Smile, Smile, Smile'. The first was a British music-hall song written by Jack Judge and co-credited to Henry James 'Harry' Williams. It is thought that it was written on 30 January 1912 for a 5-shilling bet in Stalybridge, now part of Greater Manchester. The second, the name of which is used in part for the title of this publication, was written by George Asaf (the pseudonym of George Henry Powell) and set to music by his brother Felix Powell in 1915.

The titles of these marching songs were also used in whole or adapted form as captions for many comic, patriotic and sentimental postcards. In one anonymous comic saucy card, postally used in 1916 and captioned 'It's a long Way to Tipperary', a mouse can be seen running up a lady's leg (see Fig 6). Meanwhile, on a Raphael Tuck & Sons card – part of its 'Victorious Peace Series' – the artist B Simpson depicted a beaming, bow-tied black cat seated on a bag inscribed 'To Blighty' and is titled 'Pack up your troubles in your Old Kit Bag and Smile! Smile!! Smile!!!' (See Fig 7). Donald McGill also parodied one of the songs on a card that depicts a German soldier boy, with a bloated red face, slumped on the ground exhausted by a long march, with the caption 'It's a Long, Long Way to Paris'.

Another extremely popular morale-boosting song that found its way onto patriotic postcards was 'Till the Boys

Fig 6 'It's a long Way to Tipperary'. Artist unknown, published by the City Postcard Co.

Fig 7 'Pack up your troubles'. B Simpson, published by Raphael Tuck & Sons. The Tuck DB postcards website spells the artist's surname 'Simpsom'.

Come Home'. It was composed in 1914 by Ivor Novello with lyrics by Lena Guilbert Ford. A new edition was printed in 1915 with the revised name 'Keep the Home-Fires Burning'.

Humorous postcards also drew upon and were inspired by the clever captions and sloganeering of the British advertising industry. This was an extensive business prior to the outbreak of war, second only to that of the USA, and one that was mandated by the government to support the war effort. Comic postcards not only amused and entertained, but they were specifically created with government approval to bolster morale and lift up the spirits. Numerous positive

Fig 8 'Pack up your troubles'. Inscribed on his kit bag are the words 'To Anywhere – Never Mind Somewhere'. Doug Tempest, published by Bamforth & Co.

Fig 9 'Keep Your Pecker Up!' Dudley Buxton, published by J Beagles & Co.

Fig 10 'Are we downhearted? No!!!' George Edward Shepheard, published by Raphael Tuck & Sons. One card of six.

messages, some in rhyming poetic form, were printed and distributed on cards that featured comic devices such as birds, cats, dogs, children and adults alongside slogans such as 'Cheerio', 'Keep Smiling', 'Keep Your Pecker Up' and 'Tails Up'. The cards categorically answered the question 'Are We Downhearted?' with a definitive 'No!' The latter was also a popular wartime song of 1914 sung by Arthur Boyton. (See Figs 8, 9 and 10.)

Collectively, the postcard artists covered all the formats, styles, techniques and tropes of British humour of the period. The cartoon formats were: the episodic, that is a series of captioned scenes leading to a comic conclusion; divided, or split scenes; and novelty cards that if turned upside down, or sometimes held up to the light, would reveal the Kaiser's face and features (in particular his familiar upturned moustache and pickelhaube helmet with its spread-winged eagle), or the comic expressions of British soldiers and sailors. There were also 'jig-saw puzzle' cards that were issued in sets and would reveal the design only after all the cards were acquired and joined together. The most popular format, however, was the single-scene card featuring a brief caption, rhyming lines or a conversation between the comic characters. As comic cards were also sold in France, a selection of them had captions in both English and French and sometimes in English and Russian.

The types of humour and the means of expressing it included: the absurd and eccentric; animals (especially birds, cats – a small number by Louis Wain – dogs and insects); the British class system; bullying and harsh criticism; caricature; children (the cutesy, patriotic and sentimental); demonisation; disparagement; double-entendres; fervour; flags and maps (patriotic); innuendo; irony; pranks and practical jokes; race and regional stereotypes; sarcasm; satire; self-deprecation; silhouettes; embarrassing social situations; parodies of stereotypes especially sexual ones and sexism; teasing and wit; fairytale; wacky, weird and zany; and on occasions the ugly and vulgar.

Some of the most important subjects that were covered were: anti-Kaiser, anti-German and anti-*Kultur* messages; censorship; recruitment, separation allowances, shirkers and conscientious objectors; postcards featuring government instructions and propaganda posters; camp life and training, life in the trenches and tanks; Blighties, hospitalisation and nurses; women workers in the factories and fields and elsewhere; wartime economy, fashion and the ration; war profiteers, spies and prisoners of war; air raids and Zeppelins; and plenty of pictorial jokes of Scotsmen and their kilts and parsimonious ways. Designs were also created to encourage those on the Home Front to write postcards to their friends, family and loved ones serving overseas.

Many of these categories depicted Thomas Atkins (the British Tommy), Jack Tar (the British sailor) and occasionally airmen portrayed as children, sometimes babies, wanting to go to war. Portraying children in adult situations was not just a popular subject, but a well-established and extremely widespread comic device used throughout the war. It has been estimated that about 250,000 underage soldiers fought in the war and a high percentage of them would be regarded as children today, although it is not known for certain if there was any correlation between this figure and the popularity of the comic-child format. In 1914, Mabel Lucie Attwell explained in an interview for an advertising magazine that 'My idea is not so much to draw children for children, as to introduce them, if I may put it so, with all their lovable and comical ways to the grown-up.' She went on to clarify her passion for using children as if they were adult models in the *Daily Sketch*, saying 'I see the child in the adult, then I draw the adult as a child. The situation, the stance and the vocabulary are taken from children, but the message is between adults – me and any other. Children would not understand it.'

Sometimes the children in comic cards were provocatively attired and scantily clad, which by the standards of today would be questionable, although this does not appear to have been perceived as peculiar at the time and it was a comic format utilised by both male and female artists. Some of the most memorable cards depicting children, in or out of uniform, drinking and smoking were produced by the Battersea-based London artist Thomas Gilson (1885–1971). (See Fig 11.)

Printers and publishers

Germany has a long and distinguished tradition of printing; it was here that high-quality printing, initially in the form of lithography, was developed and refined. Other more efficient and faster printing processes followed, including the high-speed steam press invented by Friedrich Gottlob Koenig (1774–1833) and later, in various parts of Europe, the rotary press. A large number of the postcards of the Great War were produced on photo-mechanical printing plates.

The German reputation for high-quality colour printing continued to attract many British orders until 1914. A feature titled 'Printed in Germany' in the *Daily Record* (5 December 1914) published in Lanarkshire, Scotland reported that: 'The printed-in-Germany picture postcard is still extensively on sale in London and at some prominent stationery shops

Fig 11 Captioned: 'Don't worry about me, I'm all right'. Thomas Gilson, published by the Alphalsa Publishing Co.

stocks of Christmas cards produced in the Fatherland are being offered', and that: 'Visitors to the Tower of London just now might be forgiven an expression of surprise that many of the postcards illustrating and sold at the Tower bear the legend "printed in Germany".' However, the writer considered that the demand for the German cards would greatly diminish, 'as people here are inclined to reject all but British-made goods or goods imported from the countries of our Allies, or of neutrals'. Britain was subsequently forced to rapidly expand its printing and publishing businesses and the legends 'Printed in Gt Britain' or 'Manufactured in Britain' or similar became a 'badge' of patriotic pride printed on the cards.

Arguably the best-known of the specialist British publishing companies that produced comic cards were: the Art & Humour Publishing Co, Ltd (active 1915–1937), Inter-Art Co (1909–1931) and Raphael Tuck & Sons (1895–1962), all of which were located in London; Valentine & Sons (1825–1963) headquartered in Dundee and with offices worldwide; and the previously mentioned Bamforth,

J & Co, Ltd (1870–1990), in Holmfirth, near Huddersfield in West Yorkshire.

In addition to these companies, there were many others who published humorous postcards alongside other printed subject matter, such as advertising, calendars, children's books, fine-art prints and posters for films, the music hall and theatre, as well as instructional and propaganda pamphlets for the government. The lion's share of these were located in London. The following, in alphabetical order, were the main companies:

David Allen & Sons (London, Harrow and Belfast)
Alpha Publishing Co (London)
Avenue Publishing Co (London)
J Beagles & Co (London)
Birn Brothers (London)
Carlton Publishing Co (London)
City Postcard Company [CPC], established by David Eisner (London)
Corona Publishing Co (Blackpool)
Cynicus Publishing Co Ltd (Tayport, Fife, Leeds and London)
Davidson Bros (London)
AM Davis & Co (London)
ETW Dennis & Sons (Scarborough)
Eyre & Spottiswoode (London)
F Frankel & Co (London)
Gale & Polden (Aldershot, London and Portsmouth)
James Henderson & Sons Ltd (London)
EJ Hey & Co (Birmingham and London)
Thomas Hind (Huddersfield)
Hutson Brothers (London)
Jarrold & Sons (Norwich)
Lawrence & Jellicoe (London)
E Mack (London)
Millar & Lang Art Publishing Co (Glasgow and London)
Photochrom Co (London and Tunbridge Wells)
George Pulman & Sons
Regent Publishing Co (London)
J Salmon (Sevenoaks, Kent)
EW Savory Ltd (Bristol)
Solomon Brothers Ltd (London)
Wildt & Kray (London)
Woolstone Bros (London).

Raphael Tuck & Sons was a very large printing and publishing concern whose new cards were announced in the national and local press. A feature titled 'Tuck's Picture Postcards' published in the *Southern Reporter* in Selkirkshire, Scotland on 8 July 1915 stated that the company: 'have just issued a new series of their oilette picture postcards [cards resembling miniature oil paintings]. Not only is the designing done in this country, but the printing also, and the quality of the work shows no deterioration from the Bavarian [German] printing of former times. The bulk of the new cards appeal to the patriotic spirit, dealing with naval and military matters ... Other cards depict humorous subjects.'

George Pulman & Sons was one of the London-based firms that thrived during World War I and the company was notable for publishing the work of Harold Earnshaw and FE Morgan. The latter's work covered various subjects and included a series of stick-like figures on postcards lampooning wartime rationing and some aviation subjects, as well as Raemaekers' *War Cartoons*. Louis Raemaekers (1869–1956) was a Dutch painter and editorial cartoonist who worked during the war for the Amsterdam newspaper *De Telegraaf*, which adopted a fiercely anti-German stance. In November 1915, pressure from the German government forced Raemaekers to flee to London, where he became a celebrity and worked for the *Daily Mail*, and where he continued to produce extremely hard-hitting anti-German propaganda that featured on postcards that were sent to Britain's allies and supporters, in particular to the USA, to encourage that country to enter the war.

Professional and social networks of the postcard artists

When not places of studious work, most of the homes of the postcard practitioners were open houses that welcomed fraternity with fellow artists, many of whom became close friends, forming a tight-knit commercial-art and social circle that was largely removed from the smart gallery spaces and exhibition venues of central London and other major cities.

Lawson Wood was celebrated for his humorous animal creations – especially post-war the ginger ape called Gran'pop – and he was one of a small number of artists who crossed over into the fine-art world through the exhibition of their work at the Royal Academy of Arts (RA) in London and other prestigious art venues. Wood exhibited one picture at the RA in 1922 from an address near Guildford in Surrey, although AW Coysh in *The Dictionary of Picture Postcards in Britain, 1894–1939* (1984) records that he also often displayed at the Brook Street Art Gallery, the London Salon and at Walker's Gallery, all in London, as well as at the Royal Institute of Painters in Water Colours (RI), to which Harold Earnshaw also submitted work.

Other artists whose work was exhibited in fine-art galleries included Adrienne A Nash, who exhibited at the RA from 1926 to 1930; and Agnes Richardson, who had various pictures accepted at the RA from 1927 to 1938. Mabel Lucie Attwell did not exhibit at the RA, although she displayed two pictures at the Society of Women Artists (SWA) post-war. Attwell was also elected a member of that organisation, which was founded in London in 1855 and originally called the Society of Female Artists. Since 1857, it has arranged an annual exhibition, with the exception of the year of the General Strike (1926) and some of the war years (1941–1946).

Away from galleries, Lawson Wood assisted in the production of merchandise derived from his comic creations, as did Attwell with her cutesy children and elfin-like characters the Boo-Boos, which were inspired by her experiences before and during the war and published in book form in the early 1920s. Other key characters were Bairnsfather's curmudg-eonly Western Front Tommy 'Old Bill', who featured in successful stage plays and films in Britain and the USA, and George Ernest Studdy's dog Bonzo – possessed of boundless energy and a mischievous although playful personality that invariably got him into trouble – who was hugely popular. As Lund observed in *PPM* (February 2006), Bonzo's 'one black ear, a few spots and his round face made a significant popular impact'. This comic character, initially of a different appearance, was created during the war on one of Studdy's visits to the London Sketch Club and in the early 1920s featured in a series of

Fig 12 'I Don't Know What I Look Like, But I Feel Like This!' George Ernest Studdy, published by Valentine and Sons.

26 short animated films that are believed to have influenced the work of Walt Disney. It should not be forgotten, however, that Studdy's war work was also popular and helped to bolster morale – his depiction of a Tommy of giant proportions taking on the insect-like Germans being specifically designed to galvanise Britons into action (see Fig 12).

A significant number of the postcard artists were directly or indirectly con-nected via the diverse range of London's clubs and art societies. These were not only areas of professional engagement wherein some sketching, drawing and painting took place on a weekly basis, but also the locations of fun-filled and raucous evenings of entertainment, which on occasion involved members dressing up in fanciful and outrageous costumes, and sometimes resulted in those who were left deliriously intoxicated sleeping overnight in the street.

During the 1910s, the leading London clubs and art societies included: the Arts Club in Dover Street; the Chelsea Arts Club; the Eccentric Club; the Langham Sketching Club; the London Sketch Club; the Savage Club; the St John's Wood Art Club; and Ye Sette of Odd Volumes. Of these, the London Sketch Club was arguably the most important in terms of the encouragement and fraternisation of the commercial artists who produced postcards.

In 1898, the members of the Langham Sketching Club – who included some of the leading black-and-white artists of the day, such as Charles Keene, George Pinwell, Sir John Tenniel and Fred Walker among others – bizarrely fell out over the issue of whether the club should serve hot or cold suppers. This rift gave rise to the establishment of the London Sketch Club, whose devotees wanted hot meals. The club was initially located at the Modern Gallery at 175 Bond Street, but in 1913 it moved to the Marylebone Road. Both clubs met on Friday evenings at 7pm from October to May and the artists would take it in turns to create invitation cards and poster designs for various activities and events, especially the 'Smoking Conversaziones'. For the London Sketch Club, a two-hour competitive drawing session on a pre-selected subject or theme – if no model were present – was followed by supper and diverse entertainment, usually presented by the members themselves. Throughout the evening there would be jokes, pranks and tomfoolery. The first management committee comprised Cecil Aldin, Tom Browne, Walter Fowler, Dudley Hardy, Frank Jackson, Phil May, Robert Sauber, Lance Thackeray and was presided over by George Charles Haité, the club's first President.

Influences on the comic postcard artists of the Great War

Of the founder members of the London Sketch Club, one of the most influential in terms of the development of the artistic style of the humorous postcard was Phil May (1864–1903). This self-taught Yorkshireman was renowned for five things: his brilliant economical drawing style; conspicuous dress sense; generosity at buying rounds of drinks; drunken boisterous behaviour; and almost perpetual indebtedness. It was, however, his seemingly effortless draftsmanship depicting figures in comic situations with economical use of strokes of the pen that would have a major influence on future generations of artists.

According to David Cuppleditch in *The London Sketch Club* (1994), May's 'advice to younger artists was to draw from life and keep on drawing from life. Observation was the key-note and in this context he collected masses of material for his characters and types.' May's style was, 'the reverse of Aubrey Beardsley's. He threw out the decorative accoutrements and used economy of line to effect. If

Beardsley was the dandy of Piccadilly, Phil May was the dandy of the racecourse. His peculiar features, fringe and loud suits were as individual as they were "sporting". Like the cigar which dangled from his lips he was as original as his slogan: "Have a whisky and soda! Have a cigar! Have a drawing!" Indeed his lifestyle was taken advantage of to such an extent that Phil May remained as poor as a church mouse to the end of his days.' Those days were sadly to be short, as he died of cirrhosis of the liver at the age of 39.

May's premature death elevated Tom Browne (1870–1910) to pole position in terms of both critical and personal popularity among members of the London Sketch Club. Nottingham-born Browne was initially apprenticed to a lithographic printing company in his native city. By 1895, however, he had moved to London. He enjoyed a large following for his Victorian and Edwardian strip cartoons in *Punch* and the *Tatler*, among many other magazines, and for his advertising art and postcard designs – in 1908, Browne created the striding man with a monocle logo for Johnnie Walker Scotch whisky. Browne's artistic style would also have a profound and enduring influence on future postcard artists, who were attracted to his bold outlines containing flat masses of vivid colour. He produced many postcards himself in this style, mainly published by Davidson Bros in the City of London, a pioneering company that produced humorous and satirical cards; one of its factories, opened in

1906, could produce a quarter of a million postcards per week.

Tom Browne's style was not original, instead drawing upon the work of the remarkable group of 19th- and early 20th-century French, Swiss, Czech and Italian painters, illustrators and advertising artists, who collectively excelled at poster art and all of whom worked and made their reputations in Paris. They were: Jules Chéret, 'the father of the poster', who refined the lithographic printing technique and colour printing; Eugène Grasset; Jean Louis-Forain; Adolphe Willette; Henri de Toulouse-Lautrec; Pierre Bonnard; Théophile Alexandre Steinlen; Alphonse Mucha, who had a preference for a pastel palette and also designed postcards; and Leonetto Cappiello, who is sometimes described as 'the father of modern advertising'.

In the USA, Edward Penfield was among the most talented of the artists, illustrators and poster designers of the 'Golden Age of American Illustration' and is considered to be the 'father of the American poster'. Many of the poster collectors during the poster craze of the late 19th century also became avid postcard collectors.

Browne was far from being alone in his passion for these commercial artists, whose work spanned the period of art and design described as Art Nouveau and was characterised by curvilinear patterns and sinuous lines often derived from plant forms. He was joined by several other London Sketch Club members, most notably Dudley

Hardy (1867–1922), who helped to popularise posters, especially theatrical designs in Britain during the 1890s; the brother-in-law artists James Pryde (1866–1941) and William Nicholson (1872–1949), who joined artistic forces under the name of the 'Beggarstaff Brothers', their name apparently derived from one seen on a sack of corn during one of their outdoor sketching trips; and especially John Hassall.

Hassall (1868–1948) was known as 'the King of Posters' for his advertising, theatre and World War I propaganda posters, notably the recruitment poster for the Public Schools Brigade, Royal Fusiliers, 118th Infantry Brigade captioned 'Hurry Up! Boys, Fill The Ranks', which depicts a cheery youthful Tommy waving his hat to encourage recruits. Despite this, Hassall's best-known and most enduring comic character pre-dates the war – in 1908 he created a fat, jolly fisherman skipping along the beach in Lincolnshire on a poster for the Great Northern Railway (GNR) entitled 'Skegness is So Bracing'. The 'fisherman' is still used today to promote the town and has become an emblem of civic pride.

Hassall did more than any other British commercial artist of his day to encourage art students, something that was perhaps in part motivated by his own personal struggle to pursue his ambition to become an artist. Born in the seaside town of Walmer in Kent, Hassall initially sought advice from Thomas Sidney Cooper, who lived close by in Canterbury and whose speciality was painting cows.

'Cow' Cooper was not encouraged by Hassall's drawings, however. Undeterred, Hassall was advised by his friends and fellow artists Dudley Hardy and Cecil Aldin to study in Antwerp and later Paris, where he acknowledged the influence of the graphic art of Alphonse Mucha. By 1895, Hassall had started a long and rewarding relationship with the publishers David Allen & Sons, who were well known for their advertising and theatrical work. The company also produced about a quarter of the recruitment posters for the official Parliamentary Recruiting Committee in World War I. Hassall must have been delighted to prove Cooper wrong when in 1901 he was elected a member of the Royal Institute of Painters in Water Colours (RI).

In 1900, Hassall established the New Art School and School of Poster Design at 3, Logan Place, Earls Court Road in Kensington, later in conjunction with his former Antwerp art teacher Charles van Havermaet, and also in partnership with the painter, printmaker and poster artist Frank Brangwyn. Hassall's school was kept open during the war years as it used a location for designing some official wartime propaganda posters. Pre-war, Hassall's followers and/or pupils included Mabel Lucie Attwell, Bruce Bairnsfather, Henry Mayo Bateman, Alfred Leete, GE Studdy, Bert Thomas and Lawson Wood. Post-war, Hassall established the long-running and commercially successful John Hassall Correspondence School. Some online sources have suggested that Donald McGill also studied with Hassall, although no evidence has been found to support this claim. It is known that McGill 'dropped out' from his course at the Blackheath School of Art. Bernard Crossley, a specialist on the life and work of Donald McGill, considers he developed his particular artistic style without significant 'professional or personal contacts with other artists', although he was certainly aware of their published work, and in one of his cards 'he produced a pastiche of Hassall's famous Skegness poster'.

An insightful description of Hassall's character and influence derives from Henry Mayo Bateman, who was feted for his upper-class scenes of social embarrassment in the long-running cartoon series 'The Man who...'. However, Bateman focused mainly on magazine illustrations and did not as far as can be ascertained venture into postcard designs. In his autobiography *HM Bateman by Himself* (1937) he recalled that:

'Hassall was then [about 1904] at the very height of his success [and] one of the most good natured of men, especially to youngsters like myself, warming in the radiance he threw out and ready to help with any little odd job he might want doing to make his work go quicker and easier. His energy and output at that time was really amazing. He worked in pretty well every known and unknown medium and as like as not he would be discovered on several pictures at once. It was all done as if it were a great joke. And he certainly never appeared to take his work very seriously, but there was no doubt the results being effective.'

Cuppleditch reveals through the recollections of Hassall's close friend Percy Bradshaw, who also ran a successful correspondence art school, that his, '...output was phenomenal. He was the most popular poster artist of his day, his humorous drawings were in constant demand, he designed nursery friezes, illustrated scores of books, painted serious pictures for the RA [11 artworks across the years 1894 to 1923 including, *A Tank in Action* in 1917], belonged to several clubs and yet seemed to find the time for fun and games.'

Hassall produced comic postcards for Davidson Bros, CW Faulkner & Co, Inter-Art Co, EW Savory Ltd, Raphael Tuck & Sons, Valentine & Sons and E Wrench, also propaganda cards for Jarrold & Sons, although his humorous and light-hearted war subjects were mainly directed towards cartoons and illustrations for advertising, magazines and poster work.

Alfred Leete and the influence of John Hassall

Northamptonshire-born Alfred Leete (1882–1933) excelled as an advertising artist, cartoonist and illustrator. He was not formally a pupil of Hassall but he was certainly influenced by him. Both men lived close to each other in west London: Leete at 26, Bedford Gardens, Kensington, and Hassall a short walk away at 88, Kensington Park Road, Notting Hill Gate. Leete produced his own wartime parody of Hassall's hugely popular Lincolnshire-based cartoon, this time entitled 'The East Coast is So Bracing – To Recruiting' (which included an acknowledgement to Hassall's poster), for *London Opinion* magazine on 26 December 1914. In Leete's version, the skipping sailor's pipe has fallen out of his mouth while he turns in with a terrified expression as a large gun shell whizzes past him. Leete also created another cartoon version inspired by Hassall for the cover of Weston-super-Mare's official tourist guides. Both artists became Presidents of the London Sketch Club: Hassall in 1903/4 and Leete in 1925/6. Leete had been a guest member prior to the outbreak of war and was formally elected as a member on 11 December 1914, having been proposed by fellow artists and writers including Reginald Arkell, Harry Rountree and Bert Thomas.

Alfred Leete packed an enormous amount into a short life of 50 years and worked as a comic cartoonist for all the leading magazines of the day. Today, this artist is best known for one propaganda poster in particular that was privately produced by the widely read weekly magazine *London Opinion* in late September 1914. It depicts a forthright finger-pointing Lord Kitchener, the Secretary of State for War, with the words 'BRITONS [cartoon of Kitchener] Wants YOU', derived from Leete's hugely popular cartoon cover for *London Opinion* that first appeared on 5 September 1914 with the far more catchy call-to-arms slogan 'Your Country Needs YOU'. This slogan and Leete's Kitchener cartoon also feature in the central section of a recruitment poster issued by David Allen & Sons in November 1914, although the overall design is rather confusing in comparison to the clarity of Leete's original design, featuring flags and extensive text including details of the 'separation allowance for wives and children of married men when separated from their families' and the 'separation allowance for dependants of unmarried men'. (The separation allowance was yet another subject for the comic-postcard artist.) The overall design of the poster may well have been produced by John Hassall, who was contracted by David Allen & Sons to undertake special projects. To date, only two copies of it are known to have survived the war: one is in the Imperial War Museum (PST 0414) and the other is in a private collection. Perhaps more copies will come to light following the publication of this book.

The debate about Leete's Kitchener cartoon in relation to its distribution and posting in Britain in various formats, its official/unofficial nature, its effectiveness, its popularity and its influence during the war continues today. Even with significant evidence demonstrating the predominance of the posters produced by the Parliamentary Recruiting Committee, the official government-recruitment organisation; the increasingly negative reactions to recruitment posters as the war progressed and the accusations of 'bullying by poster'; and the fact that Kitchener's finger was pointing to the likelihood of disability or death on the battlefield, many people continue to believe vehemently that Leete's ingenious cartoon was *the* dominant design and that it single-handedly raised millions of recruits. The journalist Anthony Quinn, the man behind Magforum.com and co-author with Martyn Thatcher of *The Amazing Story of the Kitchener Poster* (2013), notes on his online site that: 'The "Lord Kitchener Wants You" poster idea was taken up by the government in its recruitment campaign for volunteers and has been credited with encouraging more than two million men to sign up in the first two years of the war.' To date no conclusive evidence has been furnished to substantiate this claim. Perhaps this is not surprising, since the government-approved propaganda surrounding this cartoon design started in the war, when *The Strand Magazine*, issued monthly, asserted in a January 1916 article relating to the *London Opinion* Kitchener cartoon cover that 'there has probably been no more popular and successful recruiting appeal issued during the progress of the war'.

It should be borne in mind, however, that *The Strand Magazine,* and all other magazines, were not only exhorted but *compelled* by the British government to support the war effort. In addition, the publishing company George Newnes Ltd – established by Sir George Newnes, 1st Baronet – owned *The Strand Magazine* and also had a vested interest in *London Opinion* through his former employee and independent press baron Sir Cyril Arthur Pearson, 1st Baronet. Howard Cox and Simon Mowatt in *Revolutions from Grub Street: A History of Magazine Publishing in Britain* (2014) reveal that the collaboration between the firms of Newnes and Pearson began in 1914 when they 'jointly purchased the publishing firm of Messrs. Leach.'

Leete's article appeared in the magazine at the time when The Military Service Act of 27 January 1916 brought conscription into effect for the first time. This came into being because Lord Derby's 'attest' scheme had failed to produce sufficient new recruits. In the first wave of conscription 'every British male subject who, on 15 August 1915 was ordinarily resident in Great Britain and who had attained the age of 19 but was not yet 41 and on 2 November 1915 was unmarried or a widower without dependant children' was conscripted.

Conscription was necessary because all forms of drumming up voluntary recruitment – including posters and postcards – had collectively failed to muster the millions of additional men (and boys) needed to serve on the Western

Front and in other theatres of war. Desperate for recruits, the government was also concerned, as it had been at the outset of war, that compelling men to fight might alienate British citizens, which is why conscription had been delayed until all voluntary schemes had been exhausted. For this reason the government was wholeheartedly in favour of the popular magazines 'speaking' to readers, reinforcing in their minds and hearts that recruitment was a popular, patriotic and dutiful thing to do, even if there was no choice in the matter, as well as detracting from the gravity and negative aspects of war.

Leete had a long-running relationship with *London Opinion* magazine, for which he produced arguably his finest comic work. The magazine had been established on 26 December 1903 as 'A popular paper full of Original Articles, Essays and Reviews, with Tales, Sketches and Illustrations' and was published at 36, Southampton Street, Strand in London, close to the offices of *The Strand Magazine*. During the war, *London Opinion* sold about 250,000 copies a month at 1d a time. Leete produced many cover designs, cartoons and running features until his death in 1933 and a selection of his brilliant comic and cutting wartime subjects were also transformed into propaganda postcards. Shortly

Fig 13 A variant of the well-known recruiting slogan. Alfred Leete, published on behalf of *London Opinion* magazine. Although advertised as a colour card it was probably only made in black and white to save money.

after Britain declared war against Germany on 4 August 1914, the editor claimed it had been bombarded with requests for their illustrations and cartoons. On 12 September 1914, another announcement stated that, 'We are getting numerous applications from various recruiting organisations for postcards reproducing last week's LO cover – the Kitchener head, "Your Country Needs YOU" – in colour. To aid recruiting we will supply these at the rate of 1s 4d a 100. Post free.'

Finally, after searching for many years, one example of this postcard has been traced thanks to Dr Nick Hiley, Head of the British Cartoon Archive at the University of Kent. It is reproduced here for the first time (see Fig 13). The backlash against recruitment material has been noted earlier and it is likely that the bulk of the cards were destroyed or recycled at the end of the war. Hiley has also located some cinderella stamps featuring Leete's Lord Kitchener cartoon, which would have been stuck on to letters and perhaps postcards too for propaganda purposes alongside official stamps, since they resembled a stamp but had no actual postal value. However, it is not known who produced them.

In 'Round the Town', a regular feature of *London Opinion*, that appeared in the issue of 28 September 1914, it was announced that: 'A certain publishing firm has just issued a portrait of Lord Kitchener with finger pointing out of the picture, on which are the words "YOU Are The Man I Want". I seem to have seen something like this before – in a previous existence.' This ironic statement refers to the colour postcard depicting Lord Kitchener in a red uniform, without his hat and with outstretched arm and pointing finger, which was published by the Regent Publishing Co. This company was based in Euston Road, London from 1905 until 1925 and issued cards of various subjects, including actors and royalty and especially views of London. During the war, the market for producing popular designs was fiercely competitive and the company had cheekily adapted Leete's cartoon and devised a new slogan so that they could claim it as one of their own designs. The London press artist Sid A Potts produced another variant depicting a boy running away from a broken window with Kitchener's finger pointing at him from a poster proclaiming 'It's YOU I Want!'

PLEASE SIR! I DIDN'T BREAK IT!!

Fig 14 'Please Sir! I Didn't Break It!!' Sid A Potts, published by Gale & Polden.

while the boy protests 'Please Sir! I Didn't Break it!!' (See Fig 14).

Additional postcard designs were announced by *London Opinion* on 31 October 1914: 'Owing to the great popularity of the "L.O." war cartoons, as shown by the many applications for special pulls on art paper, arrangements have now been completed with Messrs Lawrence & Jellicoe for a selection to be reproduced in the form of coloured post-cards. Look out for these at your stationer's.'

On 21 November 1914, *London Opinion* announced that 'some of the most popular of these drawings [war cartoons] are now published in a series of "Twelve Postcards Printed in Colour". The cards may be purchased at any bookstall or newsagent etc. Price 1d each or direct from Lawrence & Jellicoe, Henrietta Street, W.C. [Covent Garden].' By Christmas, the number of retailers had been expanded to meet the demand. The magazine issue of 26 December 1914 stated that 'postcards of war cartoons were now available from W. H. Smith and Son and J. Beagles & Co Ltd'.

On 2 December 1914, the commentator in 'Round the Town' noted: 'I have been looking through the *London Opinion* coloured War postcards, published by Messrs Lawrence and Jellicoe … and find it very difficult to say which are likely to prove the more popular. Perhaps, if I plump for "The Iron Cross – A German Honour that has become a Shame" by Bert Thomas and "Our Jack of Trumps" [proper title: 'Our Jack, Britain's Trump Card'] by Alfred Leete I shall not be so wide of the mark.'

Before addressing Leete's card in more detail it is worth focusing for a while on his close friend Bert Thomas (1883–1966), who was also a long-standing contributor to *London Opinion*. Some of Thomas's cartoons, however, had a harder political and social edge. The Newport-born Welsh artist produced the phenomenally popular 'Arf a Mo Kaiser!' comic illustration depicting an old soldier pausing to light his pipe while a shell explodes in

Fig 15 "'Arf a Mo Kaiser!'" Bert Thomas, published by Gale & Polden.

the background (see Fig 15). It was first drawn by the artist, reputedly in 10 minutes, for the *Weekly Dispatch* on 11 November 1914 and it was then published as a postcard by Gale & Polden. Thomas also drew another Tommy leisurely smoking a cigarette seated on wooden crate labelled 'From the Weekly Dispatch' and this card is captioned 'Are We Downhearted?' These were so successful they helped to raise an estimated £250,000 for the tobacco-for-troops fund. In 1917, both Thomas and Leete joined the Artists Rifles; although unfit for active service they were posted to the officers' training camp at Hare Hall at Gidea Park, Essex.

In 1918, Thomas became an official war artist for the National Savings Campaign and in June of that year was awarded the MBE for his comic war work. Cuppleditch reports the reaction of a visitor to Thomas's farm home in Pinner, Middlesex (close to that of William Heath Robinson) in 1923. He recalled: 'the presence of two easels, a beige-draped billiard table which served as a filing centre, a large wireless set on the window ledge, one white parrot and Bert Thomas the artist – a short, restless, outspoken, chain-smoker in sweater and flannels.' Thomas also went on to produce Home Front propaganda posters during World War II.

Let us return to Leete's postcard entitled 'Our Jack of Trumps', which was cleverly conceived to be both patriotic in title and tone (see Fig 16). In it, the artist ingeniously depicts a sailor in the form of a playing card clutching a cutlass with the name 'Invincible' around his hat, thereby combining a reassuring muscular human face of the 'Senior Service' with a ship's name in order to project resolution and strength. It also brings to mind several earlier British vessels as well as the up-to-date battlecruiser HMS *Invincible* (1907), which took part in the Battle of Heligoland Bight (28 August 1914) and the Battle of the Falklands (8 December 1914), but was sunk on 31 May 1916 during the Battle of Jutland.

OUR JACK OF TRUMPS

Fig 16 'Our Jack of Trumps'. Alfred Leete, published by Lawrence and Jellicoe.

Other cards by Leete included: 'It Never Rains But It Pours' and 'He Didn't Know It Was Loaded' (see chapter 4). The first shows the Kaiser sheltering under his umbrella as various-sized shells of 'Belgium, France, Britain, France, Canada, India, S. Africa, Australia, New Zealand, Japan, Russia and Servia' rain down upon him. A sign in front on the road ahead in the shape of a hand is inscribed 'To Berlin'. The second provides an immediate humorous hit: the gunshot that has separated the Kaiser's nose has been caused by an antiquated-looking weapon that is inscribed 'Belgium'. This is a comic facial variant of the saying 'to

shoot yourself in the foot', the invasion of Belgium having been the catalyst that led to Britain's declaration of war against Germany on 4 August 1914.

Some of these cards survived the war. One example of the latter was sent from England to the Jane Fuller Club in Hollywood, Los Angeles during World War II, from where in June 1940 it was redirected to an address in Oconomowoc, Wisconsin.

In addition to postcards, Leete also created a cartoon featuring two gentlemen of differing ages seated in armchairs typical of an English gentlemen's club, a scene that also featured on a war postcard. In it, the younger man starts to say: 'Now, if I were Kitchener –' and the older one, a retired army colonel-type, interrupts with the retort: 'By Gad! Sir! If you were, you wouldn't be rotting around this Club.' Another card shows a German barber holding a cut-throat razor standing beside a seated and very anxious customer, saying: 'Vell, and vot do *you* tink, about der var. Eh?', and yet another is captioned: 'Ja! I Will Make Meinself Bigger or Burst' and portrays a German soldier wearing the iconic infantry pickelhaube

JA! I WILL MAKE MEINSELF BIGGER OR BURST

Fig 17 'Ja! I Will Make Meinself Bigger or Burst'. Alfred Leete, published by Lawrence and Jellicoe.

hat (the spike on top was a comic gift to the cartoonists) who has super-sized himself by gorging on British beef in a French restaurant to satisfy his imperial appetite (see Fig 17). The comic message can be interpreted as a call to Britons to rally round or else the German army will soon be eating in British restaurants. Another, maybe more accurate, explanation is given by James Brazier who sees: 'the reference to a French restaurant as meaning France and that of British beef as being the British Army. That is, the German army will have the British Army for breakfast so to speak.'

On the backs of some of the cards published by J Beagles & Co can be found a warning from the publishers – who were advised to do this by Wellington House, the headquarters of Britain's War Propaganda Bureau in Buckingham Gate, London – exhorting the buyer of the card not to send it to their friends and family serving on the Western Front since: 'the holder if taken prisoner with it in his possession, may be liable to summary treatment

under the German Military Code'. One such example is to be found on a postcard that forms part of the collection of James Brazier, and was addressed to Master Gerald Wilson in Hastings, post-marked 17 April 1915.

This official government warning underlines the powerful influence and effect of British comic propaganda. In a short article titled 'No Kaiser Card' in the Lanarkshire *Daily Record* (5 December 1914) the following was reported:

'the Kaiser and the German Crown Prince are objects of ridicule and caricature in various series of postcards now on sale in London. These cards may be humorous from our point of view, but they carry with them a big element of risk if sent to our soldiers at the front. According to the German military code anyone found in possession of such cards is liable to summary treatment, and it has transpired that British wounded or captured soldiers upon whom these caricatures have been found have been shot by the Germans. Steps are consequently being taken by the Censor to stop the sending of these cards to the men at the Front.'

However, Lawrence & Jellicoe also published Leete's card and other comic designs without the warning, and these were posted during the war.

Postcard artists outside of London

Although most of the wartime postcard artists gravitated towards and lived in London, there was a small number who worked outside of the capital. Three in particular made a significant contribution to the genre: Reg Carter, Fred Gothard and FG Lewin.

Reg Carter (1886–1949) was born in Southwold on the Suffolk coast, where he lived for most of his working life. He was the son of a bricklayer who left school at the age of 14 and initially worked as a junior clerk in a Southwold solicitor's office, producing comic drawings in his spare time, some for Wildt & Kray in 1904. Carter was determined to pursue a career as a full-time freelance commercial artist and by 1907 he was contributing drawings to *Ally Sloper's Half Holiday.* He also submitted cartoons to *The Sketch* and *Tatler* and produced strip cartoons for the Amalgamated Press (1920), Fleetway Press (1922) and Target Publications in Bath (1928). He also worked for DC Thomson & Co, for whom he created the character of *Big Eggo* the ostrich for the first *Beano* comic issued on 30 July 1938. It went on to feature until 1949. In 2015, the artist

'You'll have had some narrow escapes from death.'

'Rather! – I once fell out of a bram when I was a kid'

was the subject of a major exhibition in Suffolk, held as part of the Southwold Arts Festival.

Gothard was born in Holmfirth in 1882 where, coincidentally, Bamforth & Co was also based. Although not proven, perhaps the presence of this influential international publisher inspired him to pursue humorous work. By day, Gothard worked in a local bank but whenever time permitted he created comic-postcard designs, initially for Thomas Hine in Huddersfield, located close to Holmfirth, and later for E Mack. He specialised in ginger comic characters and, in some instances, literally red-haired ones, enlivened with captions and sometimes 'speech bubbles' of zany humour. One card shows a sergeant addressing four recruits. It reads: 'Number One! Why don't you hold your rifle in your proper hand?' 'I've got a splinter in my hand, Sir!' 'Been scratching your head I suppose!' Another depicts a Tommy in conversation with an old woman. She says: 'You'll have had some narrow escapes from death.' 'Rather! – I once fell out of a pram when I was a kid' (see Fig 18). The artist usually

Fig 18 Typical quirky and scatter-brained humour from the master of the ginger-haired Tommy. Fred Gothard, published by E Mack.

only signs his cards with his initials 'FG', and some others with the name 'Spatz', probably so that his employer did not discover his extra-curricular activity. However, cartooning did not harm Gothard's financial career; he started his working life as a junior bank clerk and ended it as a bank manager in the city of Manchester.

Frederick George Lewin (1860–1933) was born in Bristol, the son of a sea captain. He lived and worked for most of his life in Redland, a suburb of that city. Most of the biographical details that we have for the artist were compiled by Tony Osborn with assistance from his son Peter, both of whom are long-standing collectors of the artist's cards and whose research work was published in *PPM* (April 1990 and March 1997). Lewin was educated at the Old Trades School in Bristol before initially pursuing a career as a journalist. In 1881, he worked as a reporter on the *Western Daily Press*, although he soon decided to focus on becoming a freelance artist. To that end he submitted early work to the *Bristol Guardian* and the *Bristol Magpie*, the magazine that Alfred Leete also worked for when he was apprenticed to an architect in Bristol. Lewin later had drawings published in the *Bristol Times and Mirror* and towards the end of his life became one of the regular artists on the *Bristol Evening Post*. He also contributed to *Punch* magazine.

Lewin could be found relaxing at the Bristol Savage Club, which he joined in 1906 and where he would also have been in the occasional company of Leete. He exhibited about 60 pictures at the Royal West of England Academy (RWA) in Clifton, Bristol, most of which were cartoons executed in pen and ink and watercolour, although there were a few oil paintings. Lewin was a versatile artist who wrote and illustrated the *ABC Book for Good Boys and Girls* (1911) and *Rhymes of Ye Olde Sign Boards* (1911). In addition, he provided the illustrations for *Characters from Dickens* (1912) and Arthur L Salmon's *Bristol City Suburbs and Countryside*, published in 1922. His light-hearted drawings of Dickensian characters also featured on Players' cigarette cards and postcards issued by other publishers. In 1997, Osborn estimated that Lewin had produced about 750 postcard designs. He worked mainly, although not exclusively, for three publishers: Inter-Art Co, London; J Salmon of Sevenoaks, Kent; and EW Savory Ltd, located in Bristol.

Among Lewin's wartime subjects were a light-hearted series of 'Women Workers on the Home Front' published by EW Savory Ltd, and upbeat patriotic Royal Navy cards featuring the character 'HMS Lion', published by FW Woolworth & Co – the lion being symbolic of Britain, and British nobility, resolution and strength. One depicts the lion resting his paws on a naval gun aboard a British warship with the caption, 'Always Merry and Bright'; another shows the lion rowing at sea in a boat adorned with the Union

Jack on her stern and passing a vulture (symbolising German aggression) perched on a buoy. The cartoon is accompanied by the words, 'Britannia Rules the Waves!'

Lewin also created arguably the best wartime vicar comic card posted during and after the war. In it, an army officer (the Khaki boy) is seated beside an elegant young woman wearing a striking mauve dress (the Mauve Girl) in a railway carriage, while a demure vicar sits on the same row beside the window. 'If I had known that tunnel was so long, I'd have kissed you', states the Khaki Boy. The Mauve Girl replies: 'Gracious! Didn't you? Somebody did' (see Fig 19). The postcard was published by J Salmon and E Mack and one example, posted on 27 October 1918 to Plymouth in Devon, includes a brief message to Miss M Parkhouse: 'Hope you had a good time on Thursday. Isn't this P.C. [picture postcard] good.'

Postcard-artists' agents

The artists' agents were required to secure the wide range of work necessary for artists to be able to earn a decent living. AE Johnson was one of two leading London-based ones and also a lay member of the London Sketch Club. The second is discussed later below in relation to Mabel Lucie Attwell. His business was incorporated into a company on 1 January 1900 and it was still active in the 1960s. Johnson was a former journalist who penned a series of books entitled

The Khaki Boy: "If I had known that tunnel was so long, I'd have kissed you."
The Mauve Girl: "Gracious! didn't you? Somebody did "!

Fig 19 The public interest in posting this card featuring the bashful vicar and his carriage companions continued post-war. Frederick George Lewin, published by J Salmon.

Brush, Pen and Pencil, promoting the work of the black-and-white artists. In addition to John Hassall, these included, in alphabetical order: Tom Browne, Dudley Hardy, Frank Reynolds, William Heath Robinson and Lawson Wood. Bruce Bairnsfather and Alfred Leete were also under Johnson's management. Frank Reynolds (1876–1953) was closely associated with *Punch* magazine and succeeded FH Townsend (1868–1920) as editor. William Heath Robinson (1872–1944) was the famous devisor of ridiculously wacky gadgets and machines that performed simple functions, whose name, 'Heath Robinson', became common parlance as a way of describing something that was unnecessarily complex. Robinson was predominately an illustrator whose work featured in three books during the war: *Some 'Frightful' War Pictures* (1915), *Hunlikely!* (1916) and *The Saintly Hun: A Book of German Virtues* (1917). He generally steered away from postcards, with the exception of Christmas cards.

Lawson Wood (1878–1957) was born in Highgate, London. The son of the landscape artist Pinhorn Wood, Lawson studied at the Slade School of Fine Art, The Heatherley School of Fine Art and Calderon's School of Animal Painting. His love of animals led to him being awarded a fellowship of the Royal Zoological Society in 1934. During the war, Wood served as an officer in the Kite Balloon Wing of the Royal Flying Corps and was tasked with spotting planes. He was decorated by the French for his action during the Battle of Vimy Ridge (9–12 April 1917).

Wood specialised in endearing animal characters but produced many mildly comic cards showing soldiers and sailors near to alluring young ladies, although their over-protective mothers were never far away, either in body

Fig 20 '"Mother, I'm forgetting your advice!"' Lawson Wood, published by Inter-Art Co.

or mind. One of his cards is captioned 'Mother, I'm forgetting your advice!' (See Fig 20). Some of Wood's patriotic designs were published by Dobson, Molle & Co. He must have enjoyed commercial success in the USA judging by the large number of humorous advertisements he produced for a wide range of businesses there.

Harold Cecil Earnshaw and Mabel Lucie Attwell

Other prominent second-wave members of the London Sketch Club who excelled at producing comic postcards included Harold Cecil Earnshaw (1886–1937) and Mabel Lucie Attwell (1879–1964). Born in West Ham in London, Earnshaw was the son of a bank clerk. Known as Pat to his friends in the club, he joined the Artists' Rifles in 1915 and while serving in France lost his right arm. Undeterred, back in Blighty he learned to draw with his left hand. This is recollected in his elegant, light-hearted design captioned 'Jolly Well Worth It! Some Convoy!!', in which he depicts an imagined self-portrait of himself in uniform being escorted by two fashionable ladies, with his right arm in a sling (see Fig 21).

The Mary Evans Picture Library *Picturing the Great War* blog (27 July 2015) offers an explanation of how Pat lost his arm, the information having been supplied by his descendants and derived from an interview Earnshaw gave to *The Captain* magazine, published towards the end of the war. The following took place while he was serving as a lance corporal in the Royal Sussex Regiment in the Somme area on 13 February 1917:

'I had been doing patrol duty along a length of light railway for a fortnight, every now and then becoming motive power to trolleys for the front line. Myself and another were doing this very thing when I was "pipped". We were shoving up behind, our four hands on the back of the truck and our bodies bent forward like a Rugger scrum of two against the opposing wagon. The right arm I lost was close to the other chap's left, yet he was not touched. I was also wounded,

although I was quite unaware of the fact, in leg and back, and he did not get a scratch. Yet the shell that knocked me out burst right over us.'

He also noted how his initial emotion was one of relief: 'I remember sitting up and thinking I was lucky to be alive and I had, even then, visions of a nice, clean bed in hospital and a visit to Blighty. I don't think I felt very sorry for myself, but I remember thinking "pity it wasn't my left".'

Prior to the war, Earnshaw trained at the St Martins School of Art where he first met Mabel Lucie Attwell. They married in 1908, the same year in which Earnshaw joined the London Sketch Club. After the later loss of his right arm he played club billiards with the assistance of a screw-in false limb. He was also a member of the Sketch Club's golf team. Earnshaw's refined comic-card designs have a sophisticated upper-middle class air about them that brings to mind the brilliant work of the American cartoonist Norman Rockwell. Attwell – or Mab, as she was affectionately

JOLLY WELL WORTH IT!
SOME CONVOY!!

Fig 21 'Jolly Well Worth It! <u>Some</u> Convoy!!' Harold Earnshaw, published by Valentine and Sons.

known to Earnshaw – mingled socially with club members with her husband only outside the Sketch Club, since that time a 'men-only rule' applied. They also fraternised with members of the Chelsea Arts Club.

Chris Beetles is the owner of Chris Beetles Ltd, a commercial art gallery in St James's, London that offers for sale original artworks by leading cartoonists and illustrators. His passion for the subject of comic art has spilled over into authorship of several publications, including an illustrated biography entitled *Mabel Lucie Attwell* (1989) that drew upon biographical material supplied by the artist's daughter, Peggy Wickham, and in which her mother's anxious experiences of approaching an agent in 1910 are vividly recollected. She described her mother 'trembling with nervousness' on the occasion when she went to visit the artists' agent Francis and Mills, the main rival to AE Johnson, and also that 'Mr. Francis turned out to be a bluff man with a good business sense and great zest for life, and as "Frankie", he became a support and friend.' On her first visit he told her: 'I am not interested in the work of young ladies. But leave the sketches here and I shall have a look at them.' When Attwell returned, the agent told her 'he had sold them all and would be glad to have some more'. Beetles notes that from that moment on her work was always in demand and that in addition to postcards Francis and Mills 'brought in commissions for posters, advertisements and books, coloured double-spread pages in glossy magazines such as *Tatler*, *The Bystander*, *The Graphic* and *The Illustrated London News* and of course, much work for women's magazines.'

Peggy Wickham followed in her mother's footsteps to become a gifted artist and illustrator. It has often been suggested that she inspired the creation of her mother's phenomenally popular chubby-cheeked and podgy-kneed children, although this has been disputed by family members. Many of Attwell's character creations, including the Boo-Boos and Bunty, derived from her teenage experiences growing up feeling isolated and unloved as the ninth of ten children in Mile End in the East End of London. Her father was a successful butcher who owned a chain of shops and was probably too preoccupied with work to be the doting parent that Attwell wanted him and her mother to be. All her siblings were either artistic or musical. Beetles notes that: 'She remembers praying in the lavatory for her mother to like her, and longing to own a doll of her own and wheel it in her own pram.' Also, that: 'All of this she was only to express in moods (her brother teasingly called her the Tragedy Queen), infatuations, day-dreams and story-telling. These stories about families and babies led to her making little sketches to illustrate them.'

As a teenager, Attwell was plagued with acute self-conscious shyness. However, the turning point in her life and career came at the age of 15 when her first drawings were accepted for publication and she recounted how the whole family watched her pull out of an envelope 'a cheque for two guineas'. Attwell's commercial success enable her to self-fund her art education, first at The Heatherley School of Fine Art and then at St Martin's School of Art, although at the latter she disliked the course work so much that she left before graduating (albeit having met her future husband there). She was relieved to turn her attention once again to commercial work, initially for book publishers.

Attwell's enormously popular cutesy comic children characterised by their innocence were often set on a plain white background, the paint for which she applied herself (see Fig 22). There was an economic sense to this method since it saved time in rendering a detailed background, and it was subsequently adopted by other artists. Her figures were drawn with economy on art board and enlivened with Winsor & Newton watercolour paints, usually in washes mixed with some white to make them opaque, before being scaled down for printing. Valentine & Sons tried to encourage her to incorporate larger areas of

WHAT IS THE GOOD OF A NEW HAT WHEN TOMMY IS AWAY AT THE WAR?

Fig 22 'What Is The Good Of A New Hat When Tommy Is Away At The War?' Mabel Lucie Attwell, published by Valentine and Sons. Estate of Mabel Lucie Attwell.

vibrant colours in her work and, although initially this was not her interest, the cards of the 1920s and 1930s reveal that she did take the advice on board, probably in response to competition from other artists.

In 1936, Attwell confided to readers of *The Strand Magazine* (December, no 552) that the caption came first in her work: 'I can't start on a drawing until I've finally decided upon the title … In fact I never put pencil to paper until I have found a title that satisfies me. Sometimes I'll have discarded twenty or thirty titles before I light upon the one that perfectly hits off the little notion I'm aiming at.'

Attwell's artistic style was first influenced by a range of artists, including John Hassall, the Heath Robinson brothers and also the work of the Philadelphia-born artist Jessie Willcox Smith (1863–1935), who was famed for her fanciful illustrations and was one of the prominent figures in the Golden Age of American illustration. In addition, Hilda Cowham (1873–1964) – popular for her

'Cowham' girls with their long, thin legs and large bows in their hair – was also instrumental in Attwell's stylistic development. Cowham studied at Wimbledon School of Art, Lambeth School of Art and the Royal College of Art and was one of the first women to contribute cartoons to *Punch* magazine. She exhibited three times at the RA and produced postcards, mainly for Inter-Art Co and Valentine & Sons, of comic children, and also designed posters for London Underground across the years 1913 and 1914. Cowham was a close friend of Attwell and together in the 1920s and 1930s they contributed illustrations for Shelley Potteries Ltd for their china nursery-ware.

In terms of Attwell's substantial output of postcard designs, she worked for various publishers including Carlton Publishing Co, Mansell, Photochrom Co, Printing-Craft, J Salmon and Alfred Stiebel & Co. She produced a significant body of work for Raphael Tuck & Sons, including her comic postcard captioned 'The War Baby (undress uniform)', probably executed in 1915. This depicts a saluting chubby, red-cheeked toddler clad only in an army officer's peaked cap and Sam Browne belt smoking a cigarette. Her husband was an enthusiastic smoker and it has been suggested that he inspired the cartoon. Raphael Tuck & Sons also published many of her books. However, from 1911 Attwell had forged what would become a long-standing and lucrative relationship with Valentine & Sons. Beetles noted that Valentine & Sons reported that one design sometimes sold half a million copies a month, and that her postcards were exported to almost every country in the world, with captions translated into the respective language.

The *Dundee Courier* of 19 January 1932, reporting on one of her visits to the headquarters in Fife in a feature titled 'Men and Women of To-Day' noted that: 'Miss Mabel Lucie Attwell whose child studies are noted all over the world is paying a visit to Valentine & Sons, Westfield Works, who print so much of her work, and who are responsible in the first place for inducing her to do the Mabel Lucie Attwell postcards that brought her into contact with a large and admiring public.' The paper also noted that she was: 'tall, slender with beautiful grey eyes.' Postcards on their own would have given Attwell a comfortable lifestyle.

Attwell's cards certainly made an impact in the Great War, although by comparison with many of her contemporaries they were few in number. An examination of both John Henty's publication *The Collectable World of Mabel Lucie Attwell* (1999) and *Mabel Keeps Calm and Carries On: The Wartime Postcards of Mabel Lucie Attwell* (2013) edited by Vicki Thomas, and a selection of private collections points to her war-related designs numbering in the region of 50 or so, although she produced many other postcard subjects, alongside raising three young children.

Many of Attwell's wartime postcards were captioned with positive, uplifting, morale-boosting messages and slogans. However, there are others that do not immediately reveal themselves to be war-related in terms of subject, style and sometimes even slogan. Chris Beetles readily acknowledges the power of the artist-drawn comic postcard in wartime, naming two of her prominent postcard designs in his claim that: 'The appeal of the postcards contributed to the War effort not only through general morale boosting, but directly through recruitment and social propaganda: a tiny tot, with daddy's military hat and swagger stick points to the moon with a peremptory "Put Out That Light!"; a tearful toddler points to a recruitment poster which states, "Your King and Country Need 100,000 Men" and sadly she asks, "Why Wasn't I Born A Man?"' (See Fig 23). Vicki Thomas noted that an edition of Valentine & Sons' in-house magazine proudly reported that the artist's work: 'made it to the Western Front and were found decorating a trench, which was lost and regained by the Allies, and that the prints were appreciated by all the residents.'

Another popular Great War card depicts a row of toddlers descending in age and size order to a bibbed baby, all attired in the same floral-patterned clothing. A dog and a doll are also dressed up in the same fabric, and the subject is of wartime austerity and economy. There are various titles given for this card, but one caption sums it up succinctly: 'Mother's got no bedroom curtains now!' The popularity of the format ensured that Attwell in later years adapted it several times for other postcard designs.

Attwell's status was confirmed prior to and during the Great War by several features and notes in newspapers, including one titled 'Books For Young People', which appeared in the *Gloucester Journal* on 26 December 1914 and reported: 'We have received from the publishers, Messrs. Raphael Tuck and Sons, Ltd, another acceptable volume of "Grimm's Fairy Tales" [in which] that popular artist, Mabel Lucie Attwell has certainly excelled herself in regard to the illustrations.' During the war, both Attwell and Earnshaw also contributed work to *Printer's Pie*, the charitable publication produced by *The Sphere* and *Tatler* to raise funds for the large number of poorly paid people working

Fig 23 The background poster in this card derived from the official call-to-arms that was posted across Britain. Mabel Lucie Attwell, published by Printing-Craft Ltd. Estate of Mabel Lucie Attwell.

"The best I can do at present!"

LONG LIVE JAPAN!

Our Allies ©

THREE CHEERS FOR CANADA!

Sons of the Empire ©

Fig 24 (left) This cutesy girl's contribution to the war effort is her khaki-attired teddy. Agnes Richardson, published by Inter-Art Co.

Figs 25a (middle) and 25b (right) 'Long Live Japan' and 'Three Cheers For Canada'. Two from a set of light-hearted patriotic flag cards featuring Britain's allies. Flora White, published by Photochrom Co.

in the printing industry. Tom Browne, Dudley Buxton, John Hassall, Alfred Leete, GE Studdy and Bert Thomas, among many others, also featured in various volumes.

The wide-ranging nature of Attwell's work was something shared with most of her fellow commercial artists. She was part of a small group of gifted women artists and illustrators active during the 1910s that included Nina Kennard Brisley (1898–1978), who lived in Baron's Court Road, West London and exhibited at the RA and the Society of Women Artists (SWA) and whose themed cards for Mansell are now very hard to find; and Wimbledon-born Agnes Richardson (1885–1951), see Fig 24, who studied at the Lambeth School of Art in London and worked

with many postcard publishers, including: Birn Bros; CW Faulkner & Co; Hauff; Inter-Art Co; E Mack; Millar & Lang Art Publishing Co; Photochrom Co; and Valentine & Sons. She also designed posters for the London Underground. Their artistic technique, characters and settings are directly drawn from the world of children's illustrated books, as were the fairy-like figures of Flora White (1878–1953), see Figs 25a and b, who was taught at the Brighton School of Art.

The Great War launched Attwell's career, although her popularity was attained in the inter-war period. Her commercial success has overshadowed many of the other artists, some might say unfairly, and she remains the best-known of the women postcard artists today. There's a charming sensitivity to her subjects, an economy and softness of line, a pleasing rhythm and a muted pastel-like palette that is at odds with most of the typical harder-edged, vivid comic postcards of wartime. Perhaps it is precisely these characteristics that explain her popularity with the public, which continued well into the 1960s. Although it is not proven, it is highly likely that more women than men bought her postcards.

Donald McGill

If Attwell dominates the female comic-postcard world, then Donald McGill without question is her male equivalent. Since his death, McGill has been championed by various authors, but Bernard Crossley's *Donald McGill: Postcard Artist* (2014) is now considered by many to be the definitive work. This was published in association with James Bissell-Thomas, the passionate collector of his work who established the Donald McGill Archive & Museum on the Isle of Wight, now located in Ryde.

'McGill' has become a brand name for the comic postcard, in particular those of the seaside, with the television dramatist, screenwriter and journalist Dennis Potter describing him as 'The King of Comic Postcards, the Picasso of the pier, the Munnings of Margate'. McGill produced in the region of 12,000 designs, of which many millions of copies were printed across his lifetime. This certainly points to

Fig 26 A common comic postcard technique in lampooning the enemy was to depict the rival soldier massively overweight. Donald McGill, published by Inter-Art Co.

his primary focus being postcards and little else besides, something that was highly unusual since commercial artists normally had to diversify to 'make ends meet'.

McGill was born at 46, Park Street, close to Regent's Park in London. Early in his life he abandoned what might have been a promising and steady career as a naval draughtsman, dedicating himself instead to the art and craft of comic postcards, a decision that did not personally reap him lucrative rewards. At the peak of his profession, McGill was only earning three guineas per design, although in most cases he failed to make any royalty arrangements.

After his death, his estate was valued at just £735. Elfreda Buckland in *The World of Donald McGill* (1984) states that the German-born publisher Joseph Ascher did particularly well by him, as is evident from the fact that Ascher left an estate valued at £40,000 after his death in 1951. Buckland was adamant that Ascher profited unfairly from McGill's phenomenally popular postcards, although she conceded that Ascher did have some other business interests besides McGill from which he would also have profited.

Buckland also reveals McGill's working technique: like Attwell, his caption came first, followed by the design. Sometimes one of his daughters would read to him while he worked at the drawing and painted. His original artworks were produced at twice the size of a postcard to make it easier to scale them down for printing. For his early work, McGill received only 6 shillings (30p) per design, which is in marked contrast to the modern-day prices his originals achieve, which can run to several thousand pounds each at auction or through specialist dealers.

George Orwell, the celebrated author of *Animal Farm* (1945) and *1984* (1949), also wrote an essay on McGill entitled, 'The Art of Donald McGill', which was published in the magazine *Horizon – A Review of Literature and Art* in September 1941. Such was the prevalence and remarkable widespread appeal of McGill's comic postcards from the 1910s through to the 1940s that Orwell considered that 'Donald McGill' could be a trade name. In a Brian Sewell-esque critical style, Orwell puts postcards in their place: 'Anyone who examines his postcards in bulk will notice that many of them are not despicable even as drawings, but it would be dilettantism to pretend that they have any direct aesthetic value. A comic postcard is simply an illustration to a joke, invariably a "low" joke, and it stands and falls by its ability to raise a laugh.' He believed that your 'first impression' of the artist's work 'is of overpowering vulgarity', in some cases 'obscenity', while in others 'vulgar and ugly'. It should be said, however, that Orwell also regarded him as: 'by far the best of contemporary postcard artists [and] a clever draughtsman with a real caricaturist's touch.' After all the haranguing, Orwell revealed a sneaking admiration for the artist's work in his conclusion, stating that: 'I for one should be very sorry to see them vanish.'

McGill pushed the boundaries of accepted decency of the day and this may well link to his passion for the bawdy and risqué British music hall. While based in Blackheath near Greenwich in south-east London during the first part of his working life, he fell in love with the daughter of the proprietor of the Rose and Crown pub in Greenwich, which still stands today. They married and settled in Blackheath. Her father also owned Crowder's Music Hall, situated next door to the pub, which they regularly frequented. It has since been demolished and today the Greenwich Theatre is located on the same site. Famously, McGill himself and a selection of his postcard designs went on to be subject to prosecution for obscenity in the early 1950s, with thousands of his cards being destroyed and the printing plates seized, although by today's standards the cards appear fairly innocent and innocuous.

More than any other comic artist, McGill covered the entire range of postcard subjects on the Western and Home Fronts during World War I. Only very occasionally will you see in McGill's work or, for that matter, in any of the other artists' pieces, real characters in an authentic action situation fighting for real. His comic-postcard world almost exclusively draws upon reality and reinterprets it as comic fantasy. This fusion makes it a palatable and arguably much more potent and effective wartime propaganda tool.

As the journalist Paul Donnelley observed in his feature 'Rarely seen postcards show Britain's king of the saucy seaside humour McGill turned his hand to the World War I effort', published in the *Mail Online*, 25 July 2014, McGill: 'portrayed British soldiers in a bad light early on in his career, with cards showing them drunk,

THERE ARE SOME FINE OPENINGS IN KITCHENER'S ARMY !

stealing and seducing women. But after the war broke out he showed full support for the soldiers and thousands of his cards were sold in England and France, with many translated into French.' He went on to report what Bissell-Thomas said of the artist that: 'Donald lost his foot in a rugby accident [at school] so he couldn't partake in the fighting, but he did a big effort for the war by producing thousands of patriotic cards,' and: 'As soon as the war began he started to draw cards and he produced 1,500 different designs, which is phenomenal and shows just how much they were in demand.'

McGill was not alone in drawing inspiration for his comic designs from diverse sources, including copying and adapting the work of others. This practice was fairly widespread among cartoonists at that time and remains so today, although acknowledgement of the original artist is more often than not indicated on the cartoon. One McGill design titled 'There Are Some Fine Openings In Kitchener's Army!' (see Fig 27) features a remarkable wide-mouthed recruiting

Fig 27 'There Are Some Fine Openings In Kitchener's Army!' Donald McGill, published by Inter-Art Co.

"Why aren't you at the Front, my man?"
"'Cos there aint no milk that end, Miss!!"

Fig 28 Women often featured in comic cards encouraging men of various ages and professions to respond to the call-to-arms. Donald McGill, published by Inter-Art Co.

sergeant, whose dominating face is a very close match to one of the sergeant's heads in a drawing by Arthur Wallis Mills (1878–1940) entitled 'From the Recruit's Point of View', published in *Punch* in 1914. Several of McGill's cards that feature the same subject and that were sent by post in the later years of the war have been found, so it is likely that his subject derives from Mills' drawing. Another McGill card depicts a woman leaning over a fence holding a recruiting poster while she talks to a farmer milking a cow. She asks: 'Why aren't you at the Front, my man?' He replies: 'Cos there aint no milk that end, Miss!!' (See Fig 28). One

example in the author's collection is postmarked 9 August 1917. The caption and the subject are remarkably similar to the *Punch* cartoon by Richard Henry Brock (1871–1943) first published in 1916. Perhaps this practice was considered fair game, as many artists adapted and copied McGill's work; the copyright lawyers do not appear to have been as active then as they most certainly are today.

The Defence of the Realm Act

At the outset of the war, the introduction of the Defence of the Realm Act (DORA) would have a dramatic and far-reaching effect on the lives of everyone living in Britain and across part of the British Empire. DORA gave the government the power to prosecute anybody whose actions were deemed to 'jeopardise the success of the operations of His Majesty's forces or to assist the enemy'. The first measures of DORA were introduced in Britain four days after the declaration of war on Germany on 8 August 1914 and they were amended and revised as the war progressed.

DORA empowered the government to take control of the coal mines and railways, docks, harbours and shipyards and to requisition private land and property. There were new and radical restrictions on what people could and couldn't do in their daily lives during World War I. For instance, the discussion of military and naval matters was forbidden; private correspondence was censored – in 1916, military censors examined 300,000 telegrams; and official notices and some posters appeared to stop people gossiping and spreading rumours. All of this was a precursor to the official 'Careless Talk Costs Lives' campaign that was introduced in World War II. This is best remembered for the contribution made to it by Fougasse – the pseudonym of Cyril Kenneth Bird – who became celebrated for his pared-down economical comic drawings, some of which didn't need a witty caption to be effective, which were published largely but by no means exclusively for *Punch* magazine. Bird was a veteran of Gallipoli (1915) and survived a near-death experience that encouraged him back in Britain to create comic drawings during his recuperation. To that end, comic drawing had been used effectively as a form of art therapy.

The impact of censorship also became a popular humorous theme for the postcard artists, as did the consequences of gossiping. A number of postcards about these topics would be deemed sexist today, but they need to be understood – if not always appreciated – in the context of their time. One such card by McGill, published by Inter-Art Co as part of their 'Comique' series, depicts an army officer speaking to a young woman. It is captioned: 'You can always tell a girl, but you can't tell her much!' Another by Alfred Leete, published by Wildt & Kray before the war and also sent during, shows three smartly dressed ladies huddled together in a conspiratorial manner around a table. Their

brimmed hats are so large that all their faces are obscured. 'What are they up to?' the viewer asks. The answer is in the caption: 'Another Reputation Gone'. As if to redress this sexism, during World War II the British government produced posters reminding men not to gossip, too.

The list of things one could not do during wartime that were enforced by DORA was extremely wide-ranging: people were prevented from buying binoculars, starting bonfires and flying kites, since it was believed that they could attract Zeppelin raids. It was not permissible to whistle in the streets for taxis as this could be mistaken for an air-raid warning and loitering by bridges and tunnels was forbidden. You were not allowed to buy rounds of drinks in a pub and the opening times were restricted to noon–3pm and 6.30–9.30pm, and some beer was watered down. You were not allowed to feed wild animals with bread, since this was deemed a waste. Rationing was introduced in January 1918, when everybody was issued with a ration card and slogans appeared on posters proclaiming 'Save the Wheat and Help the Fleet'. Wartime economies and the rationing of beer, bread and sugar, among other goods, became popular humorous postcard subjects, especially for Donald McGill, FE Morgan, Fred Spurgin and Flora White.

The government effectively controlled the newspapers, magazines, printers and publishers. Publications were banned and enforced censorship and propaganda was introduced on a mass scale. A diverse range of propaganda was implemented in various forms that included: books, leaflets, magazines, newspapers, pamphlets, posters and postcards; films, lantern-slide lectures and talks; musical and music-hall performances; and children's publications and toys. Publishers were encouraged to print 'good-news' stories, and journalists were not allowed to cover events on the Western Front at first-hand until November 1916 and then only if they were government-approved. Citizens everywhere were encouraged to support the war effort.

Postcard-publishers and their artists along with the print-ers, distributors and retailers were all galvanised into action to do their bit; to create, print, distribute and sell a plethora of patriotic, sentimental and humorous cards in support of the war effort. Interestingly, there are no surviving official records of any comic postcards being suppressed during the period, although it certainly must have occurred. One fascinating card depicts an imagined British tank called 'Cupid' in action on the Western Front, pushing forwards with ease and wreaking havoc against the Germans while two airplanes fly overhead – the horrific battle subject conveyed in an incongruous light-hearted cartoon style (see Fig 29). It is captioned '"The Tale Of The Tanks" – A Story Without Words' and it is also inscribed, "Sanctioned by Censor, Press Bureau, October 10th, 1916.' This was in the month that followed the first use of the tank, the British

Fig 29 '"The Tale of the Tanks." – A Story Without Words.' Anonymous artist, produced by 'C-C. Publisher, 59, Poland Street, London, W'.

Mark I at the Battle of Flers-Courcelette on the Somme on 15–22 September 1916. In fact, initially, the impact of tanks in battle was far from impressive, with many breaking down, so this card was clearly produced for propaganda purposes. However, their effectiveness improved as the war progressed.

Britain's propaganda department

The Defence of the Realm Act worked in tandem with Wellington House. In August 1914, the journalist and Liberal Party politician Charles Masterman had been tasked by the government to establish a propaganda campaign. The Bureau was later enlarged and merged with the newly established Department of Information, which from February 1917 was headed up by John Buchan, the author of the spy thriller *The Thirty-Nine Steps* (1915). In February 1918 it became the Ministry of Information under the leadership of the Anglo-Canadian press-baron 'Max' Aitken, 1st Baron Beaverbrook, the first to serve in this office (10 February–4 November 1918). He had responsibility for propaganda in allied and neutral countries, while Alfred Harmsworth, 1st Viscount Northcliffe, became Director of Propaganda with a mandate to target enemy countries. They were ideal government choices since between them the two lords owned a sizeable share of the British press: the former, the *Daily Express* and *The Globe*; and the latter, the *Daily Mail, Daily Mirror, London Evening News, Sunday Dispatch* (formerly the *Weekly Dispatch*) and *The Times*.

Although the primary focus of British propaganda was the overseas market, especially the attempt to encourage the USA to enter the war on the side of the Allies, there was also a necessity to keep a watchful eye on the Home Front. On 2 September 1914, at the time when Masterman was in charge, he invited to Wellington House acclaimed authors, poets and editors to address the most effective means of promoting Britain's interests during the war. They included Arthur Conan Doyle, Jerome K Jerome, Rudyard Kipling, John Masefield and Sir Owen Seaman (editor of *Punch*) and their brief included propping up public opinion in favour

of the war as well as maintaining and bolstering morale on the Home Front.

Post-war, there were some writers, predominately outside Britain, who were critical of the use of government propaganda during the period. One of the most vociferous was the American novelist, short-story writer and journalist Ernest Hemingway, whose book *A Farewell to Arms* (1929) was set against the backdrop of World War I. He proclaimed that the war: '...was the most colossal, murderous, mismanaged butchery that has ever taken place on earth. Any writer who said otherwise lied, so the writers either wrote propaganda, shut up, or fought.' However, Scott Donaldson in *The Cambridge Companion to Hemingway* (1996) observed that he also believed in relation to the Vietnam War (1955–1975) that: 'once we have a war there is only one thing to do. It must be won. For defeat brings worse things than war.'

Arthur Conan Doyle (1859–1930), one of Masterman's British propaganda writers, was closely connected with *The Strand Magazine*, which serialised his Sherlock Holmes mysteries during the war years. This popular illustrated black-and-white monthly magazine ran from January 1891 until March 1950 and its original offices were located off the Strand in London, hence its name. It contained an eclectic mix of serialised fiction, adventure and exploration stories, natural history, general interest, cartoons and humour, and during the war sold around 500,000 copies a month at 7d a time.

Doyle's stories were positioned near the articles about the artists who specialised in humour and cartoons, many of whom produced comic postcards. Doyle was also an early and active literary member of the London Sketch Club, so he would have certainly encountered the artists in person. As Cuppleditch recalls:

> 'in those early days … the literary-artistic mix could not have been better. On the literary side, in addition to Conan Doyle, there was that other leading literary figure from *The Strand*, Frankfort Moore. There was A. M. Binstead, better known as "Pitcher" of the *Sporting Times* (author of *More Gals' Gossip* and *Houndsditch Day by Day*). And there was Aaron Watson who wrote the definitive history of the Savage Club (with a chapter by Mark Twain) … There were also Keble Bell, who edited *The Sketch*, and his brother R.S. Warren Bell, who edited *The Captain*. Last but not least there was P. G. Konody, the art critic.'

Some of these writers were also proficient amateur artists. In addition, Doyle had close family connections with the art of cartooning since his grandfather John Doyle (1797–1868) had worked for many years as a political cartoonist using the pseudonym initials 'H.B.'. Conan Doyle also played cricket for the London Sketch Club with Frank Reynolds, Tom Browne and John Hassall, among others. So, given his artistic, literary and propaganda connections there is no doubt that Doyle – with the full support of Wellington House – was one of the guiding hands behind the wartime articles, features and humour published in *The Strand Magazine*.

Of particular relevance here are the articles that comprised a new wartime series about a selection of popular cartoonists, humourists and illustrators. This began with the previously mentioned feature on Alfred Leete in January 1916, and was followed by articles on Captain Bruce Bairnsfather – the master of finding humour in horrific situations on the Western Front; Frank Reynolds; Alexander 'Alick' Penrose Forbes Ritchie (1868–1938), who produced many cartoons for *Vanity Fair*, *The Sketch*, and *The Bystander*, among others; as well as William Heath Robinson and Lawson Wood.

The March 1917 issue of *The Strand Magazine* also published a *Special Humour Number* to send to the soldiers, which included the comic work of the serving soldier Lieutenant Walter Kirby that featured in FW Martindale's article 'A Sketch-Book from the Trenches'. In addition, the work of the following humorous artists could also be found in the magazine: Henry Mayo Bateman, John Hassall, Tony Sarg (1880–1942), Harry Rountree (1878–1950), Charles Pears (1873–1958) and Mabel Lucie Attwell.

Sarg was a German/American puppeteer, poster artist and illustrator, while New Zealand-born Rountree became a prolific illustrator largely of animal and bird subjects in England. He worked for *Punch* from 1905–1939 and was also well known for his golfing caricatures and illustrations of British golf courses. Pears, meanwhile, was a marine painter and poster artist who became the first President of the Society of Marine Artists in 1939 (later receiving the prefix Royal). He served as an official war artist in the World Wars I and II, as well as illustrating many stories and producing a smaller number of cartoons.

The proprietors of *The Strand Magazine* were not shy in promoting its popularity during the war. This is revealed in the issue of October 1915 entitled 'Tommy's Taste in Literature' in which it was boasted that an interesting letter had been received from a correspondent: 'who is responsible for the distribution of books and magazines at one of the Military hospitals, but the service regulations do not permit us to give the writer's name or that of the hospital.' However, the correspondent stated: 'It will doubtless be a satisfaction to the Proprietors, Staff, and Readers of "The Strand" to know that Thomas Atkins, when wounded and in hospital, prefers that excellent publication to any other. At least, that has been my experience at a Military hospital, where I have the proud task of organising the circulation of books and magazines.'

As previously mentioned, it was no coincidence that *The Strand Magazine*'s humorous series on cartoonists and illustrators first appeared early in 1916. At its outset, many had believed that this was a war that would and should have been over by Christmas 1914, and as the years progressed, morale dipped. The series, therefore, was specifically designed to prop up enthusiasm for the war. The articles on Alfred Leete (January 1916) and Captain Bruce Bairnsfather (March 1916) bear no author's name, although the style, tone and content reveal them to be the same writer. The author may not have been Doyle, although it almost certainly would have been a writer with whom he would have been familiar, and encouraged – someone, in short, who was wholeheartedly endorsed by Wellington House.

Postcards as miniature weapons of propaganda

The papers and publications about British wartime propaganda in the National Archives, Kew reveal no detailed discussions relating to the use of comic postcards for propaganda purposes; however their use was organised and implemented on a grand scale. ML Saunders, writing on the subject of Wellington House and British Propaganda during World War I (*The Historical Journal*, March 1975) noted that: 'A special pictorial propaganda department was established at Wellington House in May 1916 under the direction of Ivor Nicholson' [and that in addition to artworks and photographs] 'various other forms of pictorial propaganda were also exploited, including lantern slides, postcards and cigarette cards, posters and maps.' He also stated that 'At Easter 1916, 100,000 postcards were sent to Russia with greetings messages', although it is highly unlikely that these were humorous cards.

Beyond the pages of the weekly and monthly magazines, the comic cartoons could find new audiences through the medium of the postcard. From the government's viewpoint the beauty of the comic postcard was that at 5½in x 3½in it was an adaptable, low-cost, miniature mobile propaganda weapon. There was already an established and widespread market for them, and they worked extremely well since the medium was socially acceptable. In addition, the combination of a hand-written personalised message from the sender on the back and carefully selected picture on the front ensured that in most quarters a postcard was warmly welcomed, kept and treasured by the recipient, even if they didn't like the picture. Propaganda postcards could serve on both the Home and Western Fronts simultaneously, as well as at the far reaches of the British Empire, in Australia, New Zealand and Canada. They could also be shipped to former colonies, notably the USA.

The comic cards, in tandem with the omnipresent propaganda posters (a number of which were light-hearted

TOUT ÇA POUR UN CHIFFON DE PAPIER

ALL FOR A 'SCRAP OF PAPER'!

Fig 30 'All For A "Scrap Of Paper"!' Donald McGill, published by Inter-Art Co.

with some privately produced ones featuring humorous captions, slogans and pictures), leaflets, pamphlets, magazines, books, stamps, lantern slides and films, were impossible for citizens to ignore. Britain was literally 'carpet bombed' with instructional, motivational, morale-boosting, sentimental and patriotic material.

Several notable examples of recruitment or propaganda posters were scaled down and printed on to postcards, and other designs were adapted for cards. They include the 'Scrap of Paper – Prussia's Perfidy Britain's Bond' produced by various publishers, including CW Faulkner & Co and Hanbury, Tomsett and Co in September or October 1914, and another version of which was printed by Johnson, Riddle & Co, London in November 1914. The 'Scrap of Paper' alludes to the 1839 treaty signed by Britain and Germany, among other countries, which guaranteed neutrality to Belgium. On 4 August 1914, the German Chancellor Theobald von Bethmann-Hollweg derisively dismissed this treaty as a mere 'scrap of paper' and later the same day Britain declared war on Germany. Other comic cards featured the title 'Scrap of Paper' but had different subjects, for instance McGill's, which shows four uniformed boys from India, Australia, Canada and South Africa – Britain's allies – marching in solidarity (see Fig 30).

The recruitment poster captioned 'Line Up, Boys! Enlist To-Day', printed by the designers Eyre & Spottiswoode and published between January and April 1915, also featured on a postcard and was a lighter subject in terms of style and content, at least at first glance (see Fig 31). It depicts four smiling and laughing kilted soldiers marching side by side, the propaganda message

LINE UP, BOYS!

"Sojers of the Toun's Companie," 1639
(From Kirk Sessions Records of Stirling
Dated 24th June, 1639)

South Africa, 1899–1902
France, Flanders, 1914–1915
STILL GOING STRONG

AND JOIN US
3rd (R.) Battalion
Argyll & Sutherland Highlanders

of which is clear: going to war was a happy and joyful experience and one that you could share with your chums. The fact that the four men derive from the same model with different head positions and expressions lends a comic aspect to this poster/postcard design, although it's not known whether this was intentional.

Notable comic adaptations of the letterpress and pictorial propaganda posters can be found on the postcards of Mabel Lucie Attwell, Donald McGill, Agnes Richardson, Sid A Potts and Fred Spurgin. They include 'A Call to Arms'; 'Daddy, what did YOU do in the Great War?'; 'Why Aren't You in Khaki?'; and 'The Navy Wants Men' (see chapters 1 and 5). Potts was a London-based press artist whose cards featured several of the official Parliamentary Recruiting Committee recruitment posters, those issued by the Admiralty for the Royal Navy, and privately produced posters. Humorous period postcards featuring propaganda and recruitment posters for the Royal Flying Corps, the Royal Naval Air Service and the Royal Air Force, however, are among the hardest cards to find today.

Fig 31 'Line Up, Boys! And Join Us'. Artist unknown, published anonymously. First published as recruitment poster (no 54) by the Parliamentary Recruiting Committee in 1915.

Captain Bruce Bairnsfather

No one captures the absurdity of the Great War better than Charles Bruce Bairnsfather (1887–1959), whose specialism was gallows humour. Born in Murre, Punjab, in what was then India, Bairnsfather returned to England to attend the United Services College, Westward Ho! His childhood years were spent in the Warwickshire village of Bishopton, close to Stratford-upon-Avon. His attempts to pass exams for Sandhurst and the Woolwich Military met with failure, although he joined the Cheshire Regiment, only later to resign in 1907 to study art under John Hassall in London. From September 1914, Bairnsfather served in the Royal Warwickshire Regiment, initially as a Machine Gun Officer on the Western Front in France. In 1915, however, he returned home to convalesce after damaging his ear and suffering shellshock following an explosion on 24 April during the Second Battle of Ypres (22 April–25 May 1915). During this period he was able to develop the cartoons inspired by his wartime experience, his first ones having been done on whatever material and surface was to hand while still in France to amuse his fellow officers.

Bairnsfather is celebrated for his curmudgeonly, balaclava-wearing, walrus-moustached character Old Bill, whom Bairnsfather denied was derived from a real person, repeatedly stating that 'he was simply a hieroglyphic for a most prevalent type'. Old Bill first featured in Bairnsfather's book *Fragments from France*, which was published in *The Bystander* magazine. Many of the cartoons later appeared in his wartime autobiography *Bullets & Billets* (1916) and a selection was transformed into sets of postcards. Collectively they comprised nine sets, each containing six cards that were offered in an illustrated presentation envelope priced at 8d. The first set was issued in mid-1916 and publication of the others (including reprints) continued across the war years. In addition to his remarkable war designs, Bairnsfather also produced a wide range of advertising work in his early years, for Beecham's Pills, Keen's Mustard, Lipton's tea and Player's cigarettes.

The most ardent of Bairnsfather's champions in the recent decades have been the double-act of Tonie and Valmai Holt. Their publication *In Search of the Better 'Ole – A Biography of Captain Bairnsfather* was first published in 1985 and re-printed in 2001 in an updated edition. The book features a useful 'Listing of his Works and Collectables' and a full catalogue of magazines that contained articles and/or illustrations by or about Bairnsfather is given in 'Category H'. Interestingly, there is a notable gap between the entry for *Pearson's Magazine* in September 1915, which included Bairnsfather's cartoon entitled 'A Hopeless Dawn', and 1923, when the *Pictorial Magazine* included a series of 'Old Bill Looks Back' articles written and illustrated by the artist. This can now be filled by the March 1916 edition

" Well if you knows of a better 'ole, go to it."

of *The Strand Magazine*, which featured what is almost certainly the first significant lengthy article about the artist and is entitled 'A Great Humorist of the Trenches: The War Drawings of Captain Bruce Bairnsfather', to address the nature of his Great War humour. The illustrations critiqued in the article were issued in postcard form. They are, as they appear in the running order of the article: 'There goes our blinkin' parapet again'; the iconic 'Well if you knows of a better 'ole, go to it' (see Fig 32); 'We are at present staying at a farm…'; 'Obviously'; 'Colonel Fitz-Shrapnel received the following message'; 'They've evidently seen me!'; 'That sword'; 'A Winter's Tale'; 'Never Again!'; 'In future I snipe from the ground'; 'Keeping his hand in'; 'Thoroughness'; and 'A.D. 19 ** (?)'. A selection of these cartoons is featured in chapter 2 of this book.

The anonymous author of the Bairnsfather article in *The Strand Magazine* considered that he captured the essence of the British Tommy, his character and humour. He wrote:

'In general, the comic artist depends for his effect upon the inherent humour of the situation which he depicts, or upon the wit of the verbal commentary attached to the picture. But Captain Bairnsfather, while fully alive to both these factors, gives us something more. There emanates from his drawings a subtle something – an atmosphere, a spirit – which the work of more accomplished draughtsmen, and more practiced humorists, fails to convey. His drawings breathe the very spirit of Tommy in the trenches, and by just so much they appeal to us for this reason with peculiar force, to a foreigner they are unintelligible. To embody a racial characteristic so completely and exclusively is a very remarkable achievement.'

Private Fergus Mackain

Fergus HE Mackain (1887–1924) parallels Bairnsfather in terms of being a gifted soldier-cartoonist who was inspired by his life as an infantryman on the front line, although his artistic style is radically different. Canadian by birth (pre-war his father had emigrated from England to Canada), Mackain the emerging trench artist sailed to England to enlist with the 30th (Reserve) Battalion, followed by the 23rd (Sportsman's) Battalion of the Royal Fusiliers regiment. Wounded during the Somme offensive at the Battle of Delville Wood (15 July–3 September 1916), he was later transferred to the Army Service Corps. Post-war, Mackain continued a career as an artist-illustrator in New York, although in 1924, aged just 37, he died from pulmonary tuberculosis.

There are several online sites dedicated to Mackain that include Tony Allen's article '"Sketches of Tommy's Life" Postcards', in which Allen notes that the artist created 40 cards – published by G Savigny of Paris and P Gaultier of Boulogne – as four series of ten cards. Some of the promotional wrappers of the sets of cards have survived and the information they contain is revealing. The first is entitled: 'Sketches of Tommy's Life in France – A Series of Humorous Postcards artistically coloured. Each set 1 franc 50 cents.' The text continued: 'Let them know at home about your life in France by sending from time to time cards of the series entitled: 1st Set "In Training"; 2nd Set "At the Base"; 3rd Set "Up the Line" and 4th Set "Out on Rest".' The promotional material pointed

Thinking of you all!

Napoleon said : " I am France ".
I feel the same way, with all this French mud on me.

Fig 33 'Thinking of you all! Napoleon said: "I am France". I feel the same way, with all this French mud on me.' Fergus Mackain, published by P Gaultier, Boulogne in January 1918.

out that: 'There will come a time when you may be glad to have something of this sort to remind you of the bright or funny side of the war' and ended with the explanation: 'NOTICE – owing to the great shortage in the supply of paper, and in the great increase of its price, the number of cards in the set has been reduced to 8 cards instead of 10.'

Mackain produced whimsical characters that were originally drawn in pen and ink before being 'artistically coloured' with light tones of watercolour and then printed on thin card. This certainly adds considerable charm, lending them a children's illustrated-book quality, although it is strangely at odds with their subject matter (see Fig. 33). This is in marked contrast to the sepia tones of Bairnsfather's cards, which convey what feels like a more authentic wartime atmosphere.

Mackain's cards adopt a different stylistic technique to those by Bruce Bairnsfather, although the end result is the same. Mackain's illustrations convey a child-like innocence and use a style that conjures up in the mind a happy-ever-after story, meaning that they were brilliant for helping people to cope with the atrocities of war. This is demonstrated by the fact that soldiers avidly collected them and many of those that have survived were not posted; instead they were treasured and referred to from time to time as a form of light-hearted escapism. John Laffin in *World War I in Postcards* (1988) makes an excellent point that Mackain's comic cards and others were popular because they 'enabled the soldiers to illustrate something of his life more clearly than he could perhaps explain for himself'.

Mackain also produced a set of Christmas cards, believed to be a series of 12, which was published by G Savigny. It includes 'I feel like Father Christmas without the wiskers!' and 'Our Sergeant plays Father Xmas for Bill the Ration Scoffer'.

The positive impact of humour from the Western Front

The tragi-comic situations in which 'Old Bill' and his mates Bert and Alf found themselves engaged and delighted both serving soldiers and those on the Home Front alike, and they were tremendously popular. Many of Bairnsfather's cards addressed the sanguine nature of his characters as well as the ennui resulting from prolonged periods of waiting and inactivity in the trenches. Through a peculiarly British sense of humour, his work offered a much-needed release from the damaging psychological effects of

warfare; Bairnsfather's postcards, like Mackain's, provided amusement and laughter in the face of adversity.

Initially, government propaganda agencies may have been wary about Bairnsfather's wartime cartoons, believing that they might have a detrimental effect on voluntary recruitment, but this was short-lived. As more and more positive reactions were reported, their production was encouraged, as we have already covered. In fact, such was the support for and popularity of the artworks that towards the end of 1917 *The Bystander* gave permission to the pottery manufacturer Leonard Grimwade of Stoke-on-Trent to reproduce a selection of Bairnsfather's *Fragments from France* cartoons on a range of their wares. Many of these early pieces are inscribed: 'Made by the girls of Staffordshire during the winter of 1917 when the boys were in the trenches fighting for liberty and civilisation', and they were phenomenally popular at the time. Today, although they are less avidly sought-after, there is a loyal collectors' fan base.

In addition to book and postcard formats and their appearance on pottery, Bairnsfather's designs were transformed into a mind-boggling array of merchandise, including ash-trays, car mascots, cigarette cards and jigsaw puzzles. They were also parodied by fellow commercial artists, including Mabel Lucie Attwell. In a Valentine & Sons postcard – probably produced post-war – she depicts one of her typical toddlers holding a doll standing in front of a child dressed as a British Tommy. The punning caption reads: 'Mother to Bairn's Father: "Well if you know a better 'ome – go to it!"' Shortly after the end of the war, Bernard Crossley recollected that McGill also parodied this work, drawing 'a man on the beach peering through a hole in a bathing machine door at a lady whose presence within is cleverly suggested by a ladies' sunshade lying against it. The caption reads "If you knows of a better 'ole – go to it!"'

Bairnsfather's characters were also spun off into plays and films. The original London production *The Better 'Ole, or The Romance of Old Bill* by Bruce Bairnsfather and Arthur Eliot played at the Oxford Theatre in London to full houses from 4 August 1917 to 23 November 1918, before it transferred to Broadway, New York. Film versions also appeared, notably the Welsh-Pearson & Co Ltd production that had its debut trade screening at the Alhambra in Leicester Square on 22 April 1918, where it received rave reviews. The US government in World War II acknowledged the morale-boosting and uplifting power of Bairnsfather's humour by appointing him the official cartoonist to the American 8th Airforce and allowing Old Bill cartoons to be drawn on the noses of the American bombers. During the inter-war years he also gave lectures on his cartoon character in Great Britain, Canada and the USA.

Trench Life by Dudley Buxton and Reg Maurice

Less emotive cards depicting Tommy's life on the Western Front have been produced by various artists, including Dudley Buxton and Reg Maurice. New evidence from Bernard Crossley points to the likelihood that Maurice was not in fact British but of Australian origin and was called Rollo Paterson (1892–1978). Born in Sydney, he was sent by his parents who were of Scottish origin to study in Scotland and whilst trying to establish himself in England as a fine artist supplemented his income by producing comic postcard designs under various aliases including Reg Maurice and Vera Paterson. Crossley compared the handwriting found on artworks signed by Paterson using his real name and aliases and believes them to be one and the same. 'Maurice' would have been in his early 20s during the war and he produced large numbers of cards for the Regent Publishing Co, most of which relate to the Home Front. One of his cards depicts two Tommies in a trench up to their waists in water. The caption reads: 'I wonder when the Blinkin' Tide Goes Out Ted.'

New information on Buxton derives from Michael Hauskeller's article 'Felix, Mickey Mouse, and the Comic Genius of Dudley Buxton' in *PPM* (June 2010), which draws upon some fascinating although frustratingly small nuggets of biographical information posted online by a descendant of the artist. Buxton was born in 1885 at 27, Dalmeny Road in Upper Holloway, London. He submitted some sporting drawings to *Punch* magazine in 1904 and, four years later, he used his skills as a comic postcard artist to court his wife-to-be Winifred Wiltshire. By 1909 they had married in Brentford, Middlesex and the 'courting cards' remain in family hands.

Buxton produced artworks for various films, some of which he also animated, directed and wrote. During the war he collaborated with Anson Dyer on *John Bull's Animated Sketchbook* (1915/16) and on separate projects, such as *Ever Been Had* (1917) and *The Raid On Zeebrugge* (1918). Post-war his films included: *Cheerio Chums No.3* (1919), *Hot Stuff* (1919), *A Fishy Business* (1920), *Philip Philm Phables* (1920), *Running a Cinema* (1921) and *Bucky's Burlesques* (1922). In the early 1920s he worked on *The Adventures of Pongo the Pup*. This was around the same time when GE Studdy produced the first *Bonzo the Dog* series (1924–1926). Jez Stewart, the curator at the British Film Institute's National Archive who looks after the animation collection, wrote in an online article entitled *Best of British at the London International Animation Festival 2013* that:

'It's only through special circumstances that British animation has ever been handed resources and a platform in which to flourish, starting with the outbreak of World War I when established newspaper cartoonists like Bruce Bairnsfather and Harry Furniss began to draw for the cinema screen. This opened the door for the first specialist animators like Dudley Buxton and Anson Dyer to begin their cartoon careers, but competition from America and difficulties in finding profitable screen time meant that the good years were very brief.'

To supplement his income, Buxton used his animation and artistic skills to produce a large number of comic postcards. Hauskeller, who has an extensive card collection, estimates that he produced in excess of 500 designs, a notable legacy for an artist about whom so little is known.

The British soldier, government propaganda and humour

It was not just the comic postcard artist who produced humour – it was the soldier himself. The Rev Edward John Hardy, a former chaplain to the Forces, wrote *The British Soldier – His Courage and Humour*, published in 1915. This sincere but fun-loving clergyman had previously written *Mr. Thomas Atkins* and *How to be Happy though Married*, among other publications. Hardy confessed that: 'I have done little more than select and classify the letters of that best of war correspondents – the British soldier. The soldier wrote of the things he knew about, and the result is that we can see his pen pictures.' They reveal that Bairnsfather's seemingly bizarre comic world offered a peep into the real rather than imagined experiences on the Western Front as witnessed by Hardy and the soldiers themselves. As a chaplain, Hardy would also have been involved in censoring the soldiers' mail so he knew more than most of the men's interconnected lives with their families, friends, mistresses and lovers.

In one chapter entitled 'Not Downhearted' Hardy wrote about Bairnsfather-esque scenarios: 'Frequently in the midst of a heavy German fire some British joker would shout "Are we down-hearted?" and this would be loudly answered in the negative by all British soldiers near him. Certainly, the soldier was not downhearted who pasted "Business as Usual" on a biscuit tin, and stuck it on top of his trench for the enlightenment of the enemy.'

Hardy continued: 'The Hampshire Regiment, when advancing against the Germans, sang "Pop Goes the Weasel" as each shell burst' … 'Two soldiers in the trenches when shells were bursting round them played marbles with bullets from a shrapnel shell.' Also, 'A *Times* correspondent told how he asked a wounded British soldier who was sitting on the roadside if his wound hurt him. He replied, "It's not that, but I'm blest if I haven't lost my pipe in that last charge".'

The timing of Hardy's publication coincided with the British government's propaganda aims to bolster morale and sustain interest in and support for the war. However, there is supporting evidence from other sources to show that most of these accounts from serving soldiers were indeed authentic.

Once the British government realised that humour had beneficial properties, encouragement for the troops was offered in the form of humorous magazines, including *Blighty*, which was issued free every week to the soldiers on the Western Front. This was published between 1916 and 1920 by the 'Committee of Blighty', ie the government. In addition to pictures, poems and stories, the magazine featured cartoons, many of which were done by serving soldiers. It was funded by public donations and sales to the public on the Home Front and was distributed by the War Office, the Admiralty and the Red Cross. A similar magazine with a nautical theme called *Sea-Pie* was published from 1917 to 1920 to raise funds for naval charities.

Re-addressing the importance of World War I comic postcards

Given the mass appeal of the artists' comic postcards during the war it is surprising today that curators, archivists and academics within Britain's art galleries and museums, libraries and universities, with only a few exceptions, remain largely resistant to focusing on them as an area of serious study. David M Williams first flagged this up as an issue in 1988, when he said that, 'there is … a credibility gap to be overcome before ephemera [postcards] are accepted as a suitable and serious subject for scholarly research.' He also commented that many museums and galleries 'regard such a proposal as beneath their dignity'.

At present there are only three academics associated with British universities whose work brings them into regular contact with the archiving, curatorship and study of cartoons featuring war subjects. They are: Dr Hiley and Professors Chapman and Doyle. Nick Hiley is the Head of the British Cartoon Archive, Templeman Library, the University of Kent, where work on a database of the cartoons and the artists' biographies is ongoing and accessible online, although it is largely focused on newspaper cartoonists. Jane Chapman, Professor of Communications in the School of Journalism at the University of Lincoln, has acted in an advisory role to the Cartoon Museum in London. Professor Peter Doyle, a visiting Professor in Geosciences at University College, London, has produced several publications on the life of the British Tommy and an excellent overview of Great War cards in *British Postcards of the First World War* (2011).

Of the independent authors, Tonie and Valmai Holt and John Laffin have featured a selection of comic cards in their respective publications *Till the Boys Come Home: The Picture Postcards of the First World War* (first published in 1977 and reprinted with some revisions in 2014) and *World War I in Postcards* (first published in 1986 and reprinted in 2001). They are pioneering and contain much of merit, although the range and number of comic cards selected and the supporting text is limited by the fact that they address all the postcard genres of the period.

Pack Up Your Troubles is the first publication to focus exclusively on the importance of humour in the creation and reception of the British comic postcard in the Great War. However, the Holts first flagged up the requirement for such a book in 1977. They wrote, 'The British … have a sense of humour firmly ingrained as a national characteristic and the part that sense of humour played in maintaining the morale of British troops has never been fully recognised.'

There has also only been a small number of exhibitions devoted to Great War postcards in Britain, notably at the Cartoon Museum in London, which hosted 'Never Again! World War I in Cartoon Comic Art' in 2014. In the USA, one notable large-scale exhibition 'The Postcard Age' was held at the Museum of Fine Arts in Boston (October 2012– April 2013). The museum's marketing department outlined their importance, stating that in the decades around 1910: 'A postcard craze swept the world as billions of cards were bought and mailed, or just pasted into albums. Four hundred cards by a wide variety of artists and publishers from throughout Europe and the Americas are arranged by theme (including World War I).' These postcards were drawn exclusively from the collection of the passionate deltiologist Leonard A Lauder of the celebrated cosmetics company. Comic cards have also featured in a small number of online exhibitions in Britain and the USA.

In 1917, the Imperial War Museum was founded as a direct result of the Great War. It houses a significant collection of postcards, including many humorous examples, although the collection is largely uncatalogued and inaccessible online. This leaves three ways in which you can see and study first-class examples of Great War comic cards. First, try the online catalogue of your nearest city's library; a selection of humorous examples have been brought out of deep storage and photographed at some libraries, and are now viewable on their websites. This work was undertaken largely as part of the intense and widespread international, national and regional focus on the Great War centenary commemorations.

Second, you can join one of the UK's area postcard societies. These are featured in *Picture Postcard Monthly*. Within their pages you can access the postcard community of private collectors, clubs, dealers, postcard events and fairs. The equivalent in the USA is *Postcard World*, which produces an annual publication.

Third, you can collect Great War postcards yourself. Since they were produced in such large numbers it is still possible to build up a significant collection fairly cheaply, depending upon the condition and rarity, with many available on Delcampe, eBay and eBid, among other online sites; there are comic cards to suit all tastes and pockets.

In addition, many cartoons from *Punch* magazine were later transformed into comic postcards mostly in the form of black-and-white line drawings and they are well worth collecting and studying. In a feature titled '*Punch* and the War' published in *The Western Daily Express* in Bristol, England on 21 November 1914 it was reported that:

> 'Owing to the deserved success of the series of "Punch" cartoons issued as postcards by Messrs. Jarrold and Sons … it has been decided to place further instalments at the disposal of the public. Each of the cartoons has, and when published in this popular humorous weekly, proved exceedingly popular, and the opportunity thus afforded of obtaining copies in postcard form, as in the present series, cannot fail to be appreciated by the large section of the public who appreciate a combination of art and humour.'

Among the finest regular artist contributors to *Punch* were Fougasse, Harry Furniss, Phil May, Bernard Partridge, Leonard Raven-Hill, George Morrow, Frank Reynolds, Linley Sambourne and FH Townsend.

Finally, there are plans to develop a database of wartime

comic postcards as part of a new society called the 'World War I Comic Postcard Group', led by the enthusiastic collector Roger Mayhew, who also lectures on the subject. This would enable a comprehensive listing of the comic artists who produced war work to be compiled.

Conclusion

Millions of humorous postcards were sent, received, given in person, swapped, collected and treasured during the Great War. However, by the end of the conflict the interest in wartime subjects nose-dived to such an extent that Bamforth & Co reported that they pulped hundreds of thousands of cards, and the same was true across the publishing industry. Even so, a vast array of cards has survived and remains in circulation.

The gargantuan number of comic cards created and circulated at home and those posted from and to the Home Front supports the claim that humour did indeed help to win World War I, at least in terms of hearts and minds. Their subjects, slogans and messages from the senders collectively reveal that they played a vital role – in tandem with the British propaganda agencies – in amusing and entertaining, bolstering morale and lifting up the spirits of the serving soldiers, sailors and airmen and their friends, families and loved ones. Although the Great War was no laughing matter, humour in the form of the artist-drawn postcard helped to bring people together and feel stronger during a time of protracted hardship and suffering. Many comic Great War postcards encouraged Britons to laugh in the face of danger.

It can also be argued that humour was the most effective means by which to engage British citizens in times of conflict. This was the line of argument vehemently taken up by the humourist Cyril Kenneth Bird, aka Fougasse, the brilliant British cartoonist who became art editor and then editor of *Punch*. He wrote about the persuasive power of humour for propaganda purposes in his book *A School of Purposes* (1946) and passionately believed that it was the most effective means for the communication of public information since it opened the mind and made people more receptive and likely to act upon the information. Fougasse's propaganda philosophy can be equally applied to the comic postcards of the Great War.

There was a serious intent and purpose behind the artist-drawn comic postcard, although this does not appear to have been formally recorded in official government records. Lily Breeze, one of the small unit of modern-day British postcard dealers, describes all her postcards as a 'piece of history in your hand'. It is a reminder that the artist-drawn comic card of the Great War has multi-faceted stories to impart.

If this book achieves nothing else, we hope that at the very least looking at some of these comic Great War postcards will make you 'Smile, Smile, Smile'.

1

CALL TO ARMS

On 28 June 1914 the assassination of Archduke Franz Ferdinand of Austria destabilised the delicate allegiance and power-pacts of world politics, sparking off a war that was driven to a large extent by the vexatious nature, imperial ambitions and war-mongering of Wilhelm II, the German Emperor and King of Prussia. The conflict drew in the global powers and Britain was not the only country taken by surprise by the audacious actions of Germany, which had signed the 1839 Treaty of London guaranteeing the neutrality of Belgium. This treaty was effectively ripped up when Kaiser Wilhelm approved the invasion of that country on 2 August 1914 and two days later Britain's response was the declaration of war on Germany.

The extensive preparations made by Germany gave them a significant head start in terms of the numbers of men ready in their fighting forces, whereas Britain only had a small standing army; more men were required, and quickly. British government fears of alienating citizens if conscription was imposed from the outset meant that alternative ways to encourage people to sign up had to be used. These included peer pressure and calling upon notions of patriotism, pride,

duty and honour. At the start of the war, the primary focus was increasing troops in the army, although appeals to men for the Royal Navy were later made. The numbers of voluntary recruits quickly dwindled, however, so the government had to discover the best way to invigorate the British populous and secure the required forces. Newspapers initially played a vital role, but they required widespread literacy in order to be effective and only carried a small number of pictures. There were no wireless (radio) stations at this time. So, the poster in letter and pictorial form and featuring snappy slogans was used instead to raise the recruits. This format had the great benefit that it could be posted in so many public places it would be practically impossible to ignore.

The official organisation tasked with raising the army was called the Parliamentary Recruiting Committee (PRC) and their records in the National Archives at Kew reveal that: 'from start to finish they printed and circulated 12,435,500 posters.' This number was supplemented by privately printed posters, some by magazines such as *London Opinion*, which featured the quirky and forthright finger-pointing portrait of Lord Kitchener, Secretary of State for War, exclaiming 'Your

Country Needs YOU' for its cover of 5 September 1914. In response to the popularity of this cover with its readers, the magazine produced a poster with a different slogan, as well as a postcard that featured the slogan: 'Your Country Needs YOU' and 'What have YOU got to say?' To date only one example of this has been found, making it perhaps the rarest Great War comic card of them all (see Fig 13, page 26).

Far more postcards than posters were produced throughout the war, the number running into billions for all genres, although a significant number of them were comic designs. These supported the task of the propaganda posters and worked alongside other forms of recruitment that included marching bands, films, lectures, music-hall and theatrical performances, and rallies with rousing speeches.

There was a limit to the number of comic combinations of Lord Kitchener that could be produced and consumed by the public without a counter-effect taking place, however, which spurred on the publishing companies to produce an eye-watering number and range of different subjects and styles of comic cards to assist the enlistment process. This, along with camp life and military training, was depicted in a fun manner. Among the masters at doing this were AR Cattley, Donald McGill, GE Shepheard and GA Stevens, the last collaborating on an extraordinary, vivid, black-and-white silhouette series for Photochrom Co, which also produced an American-army version of the silhouettes.

The comic treatment of camp life and training helped to mask the reality (grim for many, although not all) faced by the recruits, a large number of whom were youthful, inexperienced and had never before been away from home.

Among the many inventive humorous recruitment cards were those relating to the Derby Scheme, which was introduced by Edward Stanley, 17th Earl of Derby (1865–1948) in October 1915 and offered men the option to defer enlistment if they would attest that they would join up at a later date, although this was dependent upon their age and domestic and marital circumstances. To demonstrate that they had attested and to ward off accusations that they were cowards or conscientious objectors, they were issued with an armband that featured a red crown on a drab khaki-coloured cloth for those going into the army, and a red anchor on a blue cloth for the Royal Navy.

The government also issued 'On War Service' badges independently of the Derby Scheme, although some people wore both the badge and the armband. The armband in particular featured in many comic-card designs, with some super-sized examples being placed around the bodies of babies and children. However, despite the scheme's modest success, millions more men were needed for the fighting forces and the government was forced to introduce conscription in January 1916, at which point the postcard artists moved on to other subjects.

Men of all backgrounds and classes were encouraged to join up. Fred Spurgin, published by Inter-Art Co. One of six cards.

"Good-Bye Sweetheart Your Country Needs You!" George Ernest Studdy, published by Valentine and Sons.

A design inspired by Alfred Leete's *London Opinion* cover of 5 September 1914 featuring Lord Kitchener's pointing finger and the words 'Your Country Needs YOU'. Artist unknown, published by the Regent Publishing Co.

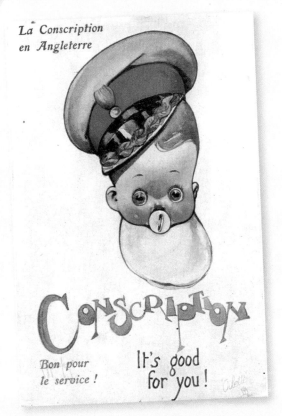

'Conscription – It's good for you!' Babies were a popular subject to encourage voluntary recruitment. S Hurley (active 1910s–1930s), published by Raphael Tuck & Sons.

Men had to pass a medical examination before acceptance into the British Army and the Royal Navy. Donald McGill, published by Inter-Art Co.

COMMANDEERED

'Commandeered'. The little girl's wooden toy horse has been commandeered by the youthful recruits of Lord Kitchener's Army. Alfred Leete, published by J Beagles and Co.

CHEERIO! HERE'S LUCK.

LEFT: 'Cheerio! Here's Luck.' A motivational and patriotic card for the Scottish soldiers. Mabel Lucie Attwell, published by Valentine and Sons. Estate of Mabel Lucie Attwell.

RIGHT: Girls featured in recruitment cards to inspire men and women to 'do their bit'. Agnes Richardson, published by E Mack.

"I WONDER IF THEY'LL LET ME JOIN?"

The comic subject of an older woman trying to find a man/husband remained a popular subject post-war. Artist unknown, published by Brown & Calder.

Producing more children for Lord Kitchener's Army was encouraged in comic card designs although *clearly* it was not a practical solution. Chalker, anonymously published.

FAR LEFT: Children were popular subjects to aid British recruitment. A playful reference to the celebrated Derby horse race is featured. Donald McGill, published by Inter-Art Co.

LEFT: 'I'se all armlet!' Flora White, published by Photochrom Co. Babies were used to encourage recruits. Note the oversized Derby Scheme armband.

RIGHT: Alluring ladies were a common comic device to attract recruits. The Derby armband is also featured. Fred Spurgin, published by Art and Humour. One of six cards.

FAR RIGHT: The combination of children and adults to aid recruitment was also widely exploited. Fred Spurgin, published by Art and Humour.

I WONDER IF I SHALL BE CALLED UP?

IF YOU WON'T LET ME KISS YOU, I'LL JOIN THE ARMY.

'Khaki – Makes A Man Of One!' Fred Spurgin, published by Inter-Art Co. One of twelve cards.

'I Can't Love A Feller…!' Absurd and quirky humour was embraced by many artists to aid the government. Archibald English, published by Wildt & Kray, London.

OVER THE TOP, AND THE BEST OF LUCK

LEFT: A pun on the command given to the men to leave their trench and attack the enemy via no-man's land. Reg Maurice, published by The Regent Publishing Co Ltd.

RIGHT: The thin, fat, idle and chinless all featured on comic cards captioned with their unrealistic opinions on how they would help win the war. Doug Tempest, published by Bamforth & Co. One of 24 cards.

It will be a sad day for the bally German when my group is called up

THE WESTERN FRONT

Of the four dominant images associated with the fighting forces on the Western Front – barbed wire, mud, poppy (although this is mostly a post-war icon) and trench – the latter as both the living and working quarters of the soldiers was a source of fascination for the postcard artists.

Professor Peter Doyle, trench specialist, postcard author and collector, provides an excellent summary of the trenches' appearance and purpose: 'In their simplest sense, the trenches of the Great War were linear excavations of variable depth [6–8ft] mostly open to the sky. Their purpose was to provide protection to the front-line troops from small arms fire and artillery.' He goes on to say: 'the communication trenches were straight and were situated behind and connected to the fire-trenches (or fighting trenches as they were also called) positioned on the front line.' The fighting trenches were built with diverging lines to limit the effect of enemy fire. Where the ground was soft or soggy the trenches were developed with sandbags.

The complexity of the trench system and the fact that men moved about largely in darkness necessitated the presence of signboards some of which featured the names of familiar landmarks and places from back home so that newcomers did not get confused or lost. Duckboards were placed at the bottom of the trenches for flooring and to provide drainage, although on many occasions the trenches were partly filled with water, a fact that was frequently reflected in the humorous postcard designs. For instance, the Rev EJ Hardy, who had first-hand experience of war, recalled a *Punch* cartoon that: 'represents a soldier newly arrived at the front asking, "What's the programme?" An old hand in the trenches answers, "Well, you lie down in this water, and you get peppered all day and night, and you have the time of your life!" The new arrival remarks, "Sounds like a bit of all right: I'm on it!"'

The postcard artists sometimes ventured out into no-man's-land, the space between the British and allied trenches and those of the Germans that could vary in distance from just a few yards to tens of yards. Apart from clandestine operations, such as spying and wire-cutting, this was an area that was only usually crossed when the order was given to go 'over the top', ie go over the parapet of the trench.

Trench conditions and the ever-present threat of enemy shelling and sniper fire, and sometimes close-quarter fighting, were brilliantly captured in the comic form of different styles by Captain Bruce Bairnsfather and Private Fergus Mackain, although for many collectors Bairnsfather remains the stand-out artist, the one who captures the absurdity of war and its psychological effects, including boredom and frustration during the long periods of inactivity during daylight hours (fighting, shelling and other activities usually happened under the cover of darkness).

The trials and tribulations of the Tommy at war were also featured in the cards of Dudley Buxton, Reg Maurice and Donald McGill, among others. They encapsulate the challenges of coping with the ubiquitous lice and vermin, as well as the frustration in the lack of variety in diet, the joys of receiving mail, and the dreams, especially ones about women and beer back in Blighty. The Tommy counted the days, around seven, before the tour of duty could be swapped for the relative luxury of the billets and rest camps away from the front line, although these areas on occasion continued to be subjected to enemy activity. Here, the men had the opportunity to fraternise with the locals, to recuperate and relax as far as possible before being returned to the front line.

The comic postcards reflect some fascinating aspects of life on the Western Front, although they deliberately mask the gritty, gut-wrenching realism that was occasionally represented in fine-art form, especially in the oil paintings of CRW Nevinson (1889–1946). *Paths of Glory* (1917), for example, depicts two dead Tommies lying face down in the mud beside a barbed-wire fence. As part of government censorship, the Tommies were covered with brown paper while the painting was on public exhibition, although visitors kept lifting it up to see what lay beneath. Nevinson was an exhibitor at and associate of the RA, whose class while he studied at the Slade School of Art included some of the most brilliant exponents of official and unofficial war art, including: Sydney Carline, Mark Gertler, Wyndham Lewis, Paul Nash and Stanley Spencer. Nevinson was also an active member of the London Sketch Club and he counted among his close acquaintances and friends several of the postcard artists.

The images in this chapter start by depicting the experiences of the raw recruits in basic training and camp life before they head off to the Western Front.

The challenge of finding a uniform that fitted properly was commonplace. Donald McGill, published by Inter-Art Co.

Physical training was lampooned by the artists but it was too much for some recruits. Donald McGill, published by Inter-Art Co.

I wonder if there is anyone else in the Army
doing anything besides me!

LEFT: The drudgery
and repetition of
training duties was
captured by many
artists. Donald
McGill, published
by Inter-Art Co.

RIGHT: Depictions of
men wearing gas
masks, as featured
here, are rare in
Great War comic
postcards. Donald
McGill, published
by Inter-Art Co.

'This puts the tin hat on it !!'

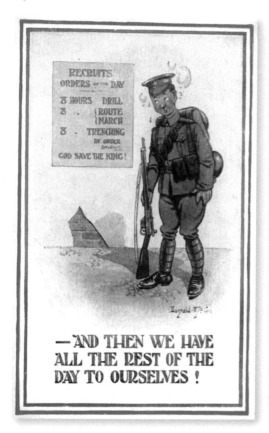

— AND THEN WE HAVE ALL THE REST OF THE DAY TO OURSELVES !

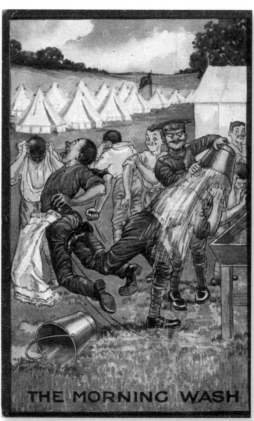

THE MORNING WASH

FAR LEFT: Free time, or rather the lack of it, was a shock to most new army recruits. Donald McGill, published by Inter-Art Co.

LEFT: The chilling feeling of the morning water can be felt in this camp life card. Alexander Robert Cattley, published by Photochrom Co.

The vivid and easy-to-read black and white silhouette was also applied to official recruitment posters. George Edward Shepheard [GES], published by Photocrom Co.

The slim and not so slim recruits experience the 'Swedish Drill'. George Alexander Stevens [GAS], published by Photochrom Co.

"Dear ———. At present we are staying at a farm. . . ."

Life continues as normal amidst the bombed building and wasted landscape with dead cows demonstrating stoicism.
Bruce Bairnsfather, published by *The Bystander*.

"There goes our blinkin' parapet again."

British resolve is demonstrated under extreme duress. Bruce Bairnsfather, published by *The Bystander*.

Keeping His Hand In.

Private Smith, the company bomber, formerly "Shinio," the popular juggler, frequently causes considerable anxiety to his platoon.

The quirkiness of the British Tommy and the absurdity of war are captured here. Bruce Bairnsfather, published by *The Bystander*.

The signage within the complex trench system is featured here. Fergus Mackain, published by G Savigny, Paris.

The Tommy's desire for food and drink not generally available on the Western Front was a popular subject. Fergus Mackain, published by G Savigny, Paris.

"Fancy being up in a airyplane this
weather, Bill!"

Where did that one drop?

FAR LEFT: A rare card
that combines the
subjects of trench life
with aviation. Dudley
Buxton, published by
Inter-Art Co.

LEFT: Judging by the
number of sent cards
of this type of absurd,
black humour it was
widely appreciated.
Reg Maurice, published
by The Regent
Publishing Co Ltd.

"Excuse me! You're standing in my shaving water."

Beards were not allowed in the British Army so shaving was mandatory. Reg Maurice, published by The Regent Publishing Co Ltd.

I'm having a lively time.

The conditions of trench life and the challenge of washing meant that men lived with the perpetual challenge of coping with lice. Reg Maurice, published by The Regent Publishing Co Ltd.

Cards depicting life at home were motivational to the soldiers serving on the Western Front and elsewhere. Fred Spurgin, published by Art and Humour.

A neat pun on the pint of bitter and the 'bitter' disappointment experienced by the Tommy who dreams of home life. Bruce Bairnsfather, published by *The Bystander*.

3

WOMEN AND THE HOME FRONT

Prior to the Great War, men were the main bread-winners in the British home. There was little choice in the matter since the range of jobs available to women was extremely limited, and those who were married or widowed were not encouraged to find employment. This situation dramatically changed during the war, however; as more and more men left home for active duty, women and girls took on traditionally male tasks and were to be found working in factories, farms and fields across Britain. The range of jobs they undertook was vast, and included assembling parts in machine shops, working in the munitions factories, stacking and packing goods, clipping tickets on buses, trams and trains, operating lifts and delivering the post. Women were given the opportunity to work as clerks, commercial cooks, constables, drivers, electricians and even code-breakers.

This move to the workplace was reflected in the artworks and propaganda cards of the time, such as Reg Maurice's one depicting women in a munitions factory with the rhyming caption: 'Work Girls Work, Make the Shot and Shell, Work Girls Work, Blow the Huns to Hell'.

It was during this war period that many inspirational women finally had the opportunity to come to the fore, including Katharine Furse, the dynamic leader since its foundation in 1909 of the Voluntary Aid Detachment (VAD), which provided nurses for hospitals at home and abroad. In 1914, of the detachment's 74,000 members, two-thirds were women and girls. Women were also instrumental in staffing other nursing organisations, namely the Queen Alexandra's Imperial Military Nursing Service and the Princess Mary's Royal Air Force Nursing Service. Only a very small number worked as doctors. Furse later became the first director of the Women's Royal Naval Service (WRNS) in 1917.

Female heroism was also evident throughout World War I. One of the best-known British servicewomen is Edith Cavell, the Belgium-based nurse who was arrested for helping allied servicemen to escape. She was executed by firing squad on 12 October 1915. Her image, words and deeds were transformed into a wide-scale British government propaganda campaign.

So women could not fight, vote and were paid less than men, but without them Britain would not have been able to win the war. The fact that leading suffragettes active before the war temporarily suspended their campaigning and switched their directorial skills to encouraging their followers to focus on the essential war work reveals the breadth and depth of the national spirit. That said, there were plenty of references to the suffragette movement in comic war cards, often indicated by the inclusion of symbolic purple, white and green colours, especially if these were in close proximity to or on a woman. Signifying dignity, purity and hope, these had been the colours since 1908 of the Women's Social and Political Union (WSPU) – the leading organisation campaigning for women's suffrage in Britain. In one of Donald McGill's Inter-Art Co cards he portrays a startled middle-aged woman standing in front of a factory gate. She has just read a notice, 'All Workers on Munitions Will Work In Shifts – By Order'. The word 'Shifts' here has a double meaning: a work pattern and an undergarment. Look again and you will see the suffragette colours featured: purple on the woman's dress; green on the door and her handbag; and white as the background colour of the notice.

McGill was not alone in creating these types of coded jokes. One anonymous card used in 1916 throws light on the gender issues surrounding women at work in the war. In it, a little girl turns to her mother, who is wearing trousers and boots required for farm work, and says: 'It's all very well mother saying you're a farmer, but how will I know whether I'm talking to dad or you with them things on!'

Reg Maurice created a postwoman for the 'Regency Publishing Series' with the heading 'War Work For Women' and the punning caption: 'MAUDIE – the Minx Mixing His Majesty's Mails'. The trouser theme is continued in one of Fred Spurgin's most ardent designs, which depicts an attractive woman in a munitions factory. She proudly stands in dungarees defiantly confronting the viewer. The caption reads: 'Nervous? – Not in these trousers!'.

Men who were too old or unfit for active service and children also featured on cards, along with imagined families such as the Dams. This extended family of war workers of various ages and expertise were unified by patriotic duty 'to do their bit'. The Dam family was nothing new in the war, having first emerged in printed formats, including postcard, in the late 19th century and inspired a popular US comedy film *The Whole Dam Family and the Dam Dog* (1905) directed by Edwin S Porter. In the film, each family member is introduced with a close-up and a name card, a trope that is echoed in the Great War comic cards.

Women were never far away from many of the other comic-postcard subjects of life on the Home Front, including: conscientious objectors and shirkers; nurses and servicemen in their hospital blues; wartime economy; fashion; rationing; and the comic situations experienced by Scotsmen on leave.

Comic cards featuring women in trousers remained popular in the 1910s, 1920s and 1930s. Fred Spurgin, published anonymously as 'Series No 361'. One of a series of six.

A play on words on work shifts and shifts that were also under-garments. Donald McGill, published by Inter-Art Co.

WAR WORK FOR WOMEN.

MAUDIE—
the Minx
Mixing
His Majesty's
Mails.

THUMBS UP!

FAR LEFT: 'Maudie the Minx'. Rhyming captions to cards were a popular comic device. Reg Maurice, published by The Regent Publishing Co Ltd.

LEFT: The 'Thumbs Up!' of approval from a Tommy to the war work adopted by women normally associated with men. Fred Spurgin, published by Art and Humour.

The change of gender roles caused confusion to some children according to this comic card. Artist unknown (signed with WF monogram), published as part of the 'HB Series'.

An alluring lady (nicknamed a bomb or bombshell) encourages men to respond to the call to arms. Her Derby Scheme armlet features a heart rather than a crown. Artist unknown, published by the City Postcard Co, series 487.

The whole Dam family!

LEFT: Families were a popular comic device to depict solidarity and unity in wartime. 'The whole Dam family!' was inspired by a popular US comic film. Donald McGill (top) and Adrienne A Nash (bottom), both published by Inter-Art Co.

BELOW: One of the functions of the Special Constables was to prevent the enemy from interfering with the nation's water supply. Thomas Gilson, published anonymously and inscribed 'No 609'.

WE'RE ALL DOING OUR LITTLE BIT!

"Every Copper Helps."

The Salute.

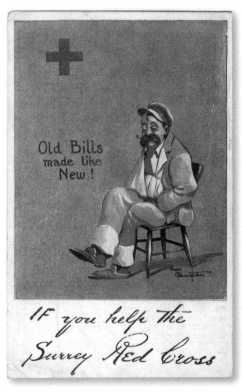

Old Bills made like New!

IF you help the Surrey Red Cross

Attwell's imaginary toy-land world briefly diverts attention away from the real hardships experienced by wounded servicemen. Mabel Lucie Attwell, published by the Carlton Publishing Co. Estate of Mabel Lucie Attwell.

A pun on Bairnsfather's popular trench character 'Old Bill'. Bruce Bairnsfather, published on behalf of the British Red Cross, Surrey Branch.

The Slacker.

WHO'S AFRAID?

Dickie the slacker in the foreground is isolated, whilst William the serving soldier is happily escorted by Rachel. HGC Marsh-Lambert, published by CW Faulkner & Co.

A rare depiction of the infamous white feather given out by women, many of whom were suffragettes, to men they considered to be cowards. George Ernest Studdy, published by James Henderson & Sons.

Whether or not the attempts to shame conscientious objectors into taking an active service role worked is uncertain.
Archibald English, published as part of the 'HB Series'.

Food shortages stemmed from the relentless German U-boat campaign, although those in the country were not short of eggs. Doug Tempest, published by Bamforth & Co.

Sugar was the first item to be rationed in January 1918. By the end of April meat, butter, cheese and margarine were also rationed. Donald McGill, published by Inter-Art Co.

'Both British Bre(a)d'. A card encouraging Britons to appreciate their own 'productions' and create more. Artist unknown, published by The Regent Publishing Co Ltd.

Britons queue in the policed line to buy potatoes. In 1916 the potato crop in Scotland and parts of England had failed, adding to the difficulties of supply. Reg Maurice, published by Wildt & Kray.

WAR TIME ECONOMY.

"Economy in Clothes!"

"I'M A WEE BIT SHORT."

FAR LEFT: Extravagant dress, as depicted by the girl here, was deemed by the government to be detrimental to the war effort. Flora White, published by E Mack.

LEFT: Many cards poked fun at the Scottish soldier's kilt. This one is a wee bit economical. Reg Maurice, published by The Regent Publishing Co Ltd.

4

POKING FUN AT THE ENEMY

The British Museum's 'Propaganda: Power and Persuasion' exhibition held in May–September 2013 was a timely reminder of propaganda's awesome global influence, especially in relation to how it was used in the Great War. Running alongside the campaigns to ensure that citizens acted upon and obeyed specific instructions, rules and regulations was another campaign with a specifically darker purpose: to demonise and ridicule our enemies. There were some cards directed at the Turks but the three main targets were: Kaiser Wilhelm II and his family; German soldiers; and their *Kultur* – that is German civilisation and culture, something that the Fatherland believed to be superior.

Drawing upon a brilliant British artistic and literary legacy of cutting satirical humour, the postcard artists set to work in tandem with the poster designers and film-makers. Their work was supported by writers who were tasked to produce articles for newspapers and magazines and text for public speeches. As a potent weapon, propaganda had to be handled carefully to be of use; if there was too little it would be ineffective, too much and the audience would question the rationale behind it and perhaps rebut it.

For the comic-card artists, the quest was to seek out the key characteristics that set the Germans apart from us – the things that they admired, enjoyed and relished that could be manipulated so that they appeared alien and unattractive. The artists did not have to look further than the official uniforms worn by the Kaiser and his soldiers to find rich seams of comic relief and reasons to pour scorn. In particular the Kaiser's ludicrous-looking pickelhaube helmet topped with the spiked top or large spread-winged eagle, the pompous Imperial draped cape and the upturned eccentric moustache, were easy pickings.

As the war progressed, the images became increasingly brutal and moved away from mainstream popular humour. Common tropes included showing the Kaiser, or one or more of his army, being scolded by John Bull, harassed by French poodles, hounded by British bulldogs and mauled by Russian bears. The Germans were depicted as asses, eagles, geese, goats, pigs, rabbits, rats, spiders and vultures, while the German Emperor was a mad dog or

Little Jack Horner placed in a corner, where he cried like a baby. He was the devil incarnate who needed swatting in the form of a fly to prevent him from achieving his aim of global domination and the enslavement of the British people and her allies. There were reversible novelty cards or 'fantasy heads', which held one way show a traditional portrait of the Kaiser, but turned upside down reveal a very different image.

A particular favourite visual metaphor of the humorous artists was the sausage, or perhaps that should be *bratwurst*. In some, the Kaiser's head, arms and legs extend from a super-sized sausage, sometimes with sauerkraut and lager featuring in the background. In others, the Kaiser-sausage becomes Humpty-Dumpty and is shattered as a result of his great fall, the intentional double-meaning being that the Kaiser too would suffer a great fall from power. The Kaiser was the broken German toy and the turkey about to be cooked in one of Kitchener's ovens. He's the man who accidentally blew his nose off with an antiquated weapon inscribed 'Belgium'. One design attributed to Fred Spurgin shows a group of Germans of various ages, heights and sizes standing before an official German poster in Sausage Strasse with some wearing the pickelhaube. They are a mostly dim-witted, bespectacled lot with a chubby Bavarian pipe-smoker at the fore, by whose feet lies a dachshund, the German short-legged sausage dog and a symbol of Germany that was reviled throughout the war. The poster proclaims: 'We are all Germans Gott Help US!!'

IT NEVER RAINS BUT IT POURS

Kaiser Bill is 'rained' on by Britain and her allies with artillery shells encouraging him and his armies to return to Berlin. Alfred Leete, published by Lawrence and Jellicoe.

HE DIDN'T KNOW IT WAS LOADED

A caricature of the Kaiser who shoots his own nose off by pulling the trigger of the Belgium gun. Alfred Leete, published by Lawrence and Jellicoe.

AN INDIAN REVERSE FOR THE KAISER.

IN THE DARDAN-OH! 'ELL-ES!!
EN PLEIN DANS LES DARDANELLES!

Turn this card of a turbaned Indian soldier upside down and the gloomy face of the Kaiser appears. The Indian Army was one of the largest volunteer forces fighting for Britain and her allies. Signed with the monogram WF, published anonymously.

In comparison to comic card subjects featuring Germans, those relating to Turks were not as popular probably because of the embarrassing failure of the British and allied Gallipoli campaign in the Dardanelles. Donald McGill, published by Inter-Art Co.

A popular Victorian child's toy demonstrates the dramatic rise and crushing fall of the Kaiser. Artist unknown, published by The Regent Publishing Co Ltd.

The pickelhaube presented easy pickings for the comic artists. A dramatic eagle dominates the child's helmet. Fred Spurgin, published by Inter-Art Co.

NOBODY LOVES ME.

"EVERYBODY'S
LOVED BY SOMEONE."

FAR LEFT: The Kaiser was often depicted as being isolated and unloved. George Alexander Stevens [GAS], published by Photochrom Co.

LEFT: Love for the Kaiser did come from one significant source – the devil. Donald McGill, published by Inter-Art Co.

NO BILL, WE 'AINT SEEN YOUR TURKEY.

John Bull and his allied chums infuriate Kaiser Bill by eating his turkey, a double play on the German ally Turkey. ES Taylor (active 1910s-1930s), published by E Mack. Taylor produced cards for various publishers including Brown and Calder.

This tank has been transformed into a mechanical British bulldog. George Edward Shepheard [GES], published by Raphael Tuck and Sons. One of three cards.

DOING HIS LITTLE BIT.

The propaganda message here is that even a boy scout can capture hapless German soldiers and a Zeppelin. Harold Earnshaw, published by Valentine and Sons.

Has anyone seen a German Band?

"ANYHOW—IT WAS MADE IN GERMANY!"

The bandaged British bulldog has clearly been active in battle and he's eaten the German band. William Stocker Shaw, published by Woolstone Bros (The Milton Postcard).

As the war progressed anything made in Germany was shunned in favour of British or allied goods. Artist unknown, published by J Salmon, Sevenoaks.

WELL, HE LOOKS A BIT BIG, BUT HE'LL JUST ABOUT MAKE A MEAL FOR THE THREE OF US!

The British bulldog, the Russian bear and the French poodle ponder the German sausage. Despite its large size together they will devour it. Donald McGill, published by Inter-Art Co.

Four of the German things that British card artists attacked come together in this card design: the pickelhaube, sauerkraut, sausage and lager. Attributed to Reg Maurice, published by The Regent Publishing Co Ltd.

'Gott [God] Help Us!!' depicts gormless Germans of various ages and sizes with a German 'sausage dog' in Sausage Strasse (street) in front of an imagined official poster. Attributed to Fred Spurgin, published by Inter-Art Co.

5

WAR AT SEA

Jack Tar is the slang name for sailors of the British Royal Navy and merchant service, although the term was also used in the United States. Like Tommy Atkins, Jack Tar was often depicted in a negative way during times of peace. In action, however, he was the ideal morale-boosting, patriotic icon – a figure of cheerful resolve and gritty determination and strength in practically every artistic format, even when poking fun at himself or being mocked by others.

The origins of Jack Tar are unknown, but Jack was and remains a popular name and tar was commonplace aboard ships, so it is not strange that the two were paired together. As an adaptable and popular comic figure, Jack Tar fully emerged in Britain in the second half of the 18th century in literature and in caricatures. Beyond representing a British sailor, or the Royal Navy, Jack also symbolises Britain – he's the maritime equivalent to John Bull.

Jack Tar in postcard form is rarely depicted fighting in specific sea battles during the Great War. In any case, these were few in number – the Battle of Jutland (31 May–1 June 1916) being the only major battleship action of the period. During this battle, the British Royal Navy's Grand Fleet under

Admiral Sir John Jellicoe took on the Imperial German Navy's High Seas Fleet under Vice-Admiral Reinhard Scheer in the North Sea, close to the Jutland Peninsula of Denmark. However, far from being another Trafalgar triumph, this was not an action that Britain wanted to remember; the meeting of state-of-the-art British *Dreadnought* ships that had been developed prior to the war and their German equivalents resulted in a stalemate, but the British casualties were far higher in terms of men and ships.

Britannia no longer ruled the waves, although censorship prevented this fact from being immediately known back home. Instead, the government encouraged the production of comic cards that projected positive images of Jack Tar. He alone, or in company with his mates, was featured standing or sitting in, on, or by the shipboard guns, or dancing arm-in-arm with ladies symbolising some of Britain's allies, the colours of their respective flags incorporated into their clothes, and some captioned: 'We all love Jack'.

Jack was sometimes depicted as being slightly stupid, although for the most part good-natured and well-intentioned. His actions and demeanour were reassuring and his happy-go-lucky, nonchalant manner was ideal for projecting a carefree defiance to the British people, her allies and enemies. This can be seen in a postcard that portrays a chubby, dim-witted Jack reading the front page of 'The Daily Snort' with the headline 'Where are the U-Boats???' The caption reads: 'What's the use of asking me – I'm only a gunner, not a bally diver!' Yet another design issued in both English and French plays on the word 'mine' and features a girl with a portrait of her Jack Tar beside her reading a newsboard featuring the headline: 'Mines in the North Sea'. She exclaims: 'So's Mine!'

Germany, meanwhile, turned its attention away from battleships to submarine warfare in the form of the U-boat. Both the actual and the perceived threat posed by these vessels also became the subject of comic cards, although real actions and situations were generally not shown. One of these was created by London-born Ernest Noble, whose quirky card shows a child perched precariously on the top of a German U-boat periscope with a British steamship visible on the horizon. How the child got there is not explained.

The submarine threat almost brought Britain to her knees by cutting off vital overseas supplies, and one of the turning points in the war was the sinking of the British ocean liner RMS *Lusitania* on 7 May 1915. This Cunard steamship had sailed from New York and was approaching the Old Head of Kinsale in southern Ireland when she was struck by a torpedo fired from the German U-boat *U-20*. Around 1,200 people lost their lives, including 128 American citizens, a casualty figure that in time would encourage the USA to enter the war in support of Britain and her allies as an associate power. Propaganda posters, pictures and medallions were created in response to this atrocity, although they were horrific rather than comic in nature.

Donald McGill created many of his finest Royal Navy-related cards for Inter-Art Co. On one propaganda design he depicts a boy holding a telescope aboard a battleship with the name HMS *Victory* on his cap tally. The caption is in rhyming form: 'What has England Got to Fear, When Me An' Jellicoe Are Here!' Another McGill card design shows six Jack Tars of various ages and sizes. The names on their caps: HMS *Apollo*, HMS *Hercules*, HMS *Implacable*, HMS *Terrible*, HMS *Venerable* and HMS *Fairy* being determined by their appearance and facial expression. For instance, the *Venerable* is a child and the *Fairy* is a man resembling a bulldog. The card is captioned 'What's in a name, anyway?'

The bulldog was a popular comic device for the artists. One anonymous card, published as part of the 'Valentine's Series' and postmarked 23 September 1914, depicts a bulldog with HMS *England* inscribed on his cap tally and a Union Jack flag below. The message reads: 'I've a hearty grip for a friend, and a heartier GRIP for a foe, and he that would cast England down has a mighty rough road to go!'

WE ALL LOVE JACK.

A show of Royal Navy unity with Jack dancing alongside allied partners of Japan, France, Russia and Belgium. Fred Spurgin, published by Inter-Art Co.

DREAD-NOUGHTS.

'Dread-noughts' is a play on the name of the British battleship HMS *Dreadnought* (1906) and a ship that revolutionised naval power. They became a symbol of national power. Fred Spurgin, published by Inter-Art Co.

WHO'S AFRAID?

Uniformed children in imagined wartime situations were one of the most popular wartime comic tropes of the postcard artists. Fred Spurgin, published by Inter-Art Co.

Damn these U Boats.

WHAT HAS ENGLAND
GOT TO FEAR
WHEN ME 'AN' JELLICOE
ARE HERE !

"Que peut craindre l'Angleterre quand Jellicoe et
moi nous sommes la ? "

The German U-boat threat almost brought Britain to her knees in 1917. How the baby perched on top of the enemy periscope got there is not explained! Ernest Noble, published anonymously as 'Series No 939'.

Admiral John Rushworth Jellicoe, 1st Earl Jellicoe (1859–1935) commanded the Grand Fleet at the Battle of Jutland (31 May–1 June 1916). The British public were disappointed no Trafalgar-style victory was won. Donald McGill, published by Inter-Art Co.

What's in a name, anyway?

The sailors' faces are at odds with the meaning of the ships' names indicated on their cap tallies. Donald McGill, published by Inter-Art Co.

"EVERY·INCH·A·MAN"

HMS *Lion* (1910) was the flagship of the Grand Fleet's battlecruisers. The lined-up 'cubs' wouldn't last long in a real sea battle! Donald McGill, published by Inter-Art Co.

The influence of the suffragettes and the fashion designer Paul Poiret are evident in this card depicting a woman in a sailor suit and a man in a dress. Examples of this card were posted before and during the war. Reg Carter, published by Valentine and Sons.

A British bulldog with HMS *England* inscribed on his cap tally. The dog derives from a photographic source, published by Valentine and Sons.

SO DO WE !!!

"I'm sure I like soldiers best!"
"J'aimerais mieux un soldat qu'un marin!"

'The Navy Wants Men' was a real recruitment poster. The response of the children behaving as adults is imagined. Sid A Potts, published by Gale & Polden. The poster was produced by 'the Admiralty Recruiting Department WH Smith and Sons, Printers, 55 Fetter Lane, London, EC'.

'"I'm sure I like soldiers best!"' Competition between the military services was encouraged in comic card subjects. Agnes Richardson, published by Inter-Art Co.

A BOLT FROM THE BLUE.

"SAY WHEN!"

FAR LEFT: Note the giant lion-like hands and feet of the sailor who wrestles the shell with an 'endearing note' for the enemy to the gun. George Ernest Studdy, published by Valentine and Sons.

LEFT: The gargantuan gormless sailor balances two shells under each arm. His dedication to his task in hand cannot be faulted. Attributed to Fred Spurgin, published by Inter-Art Co.

'Are We Downhearted…' was a popular World War I song sung by Arthur Boyton. George Edward Shepheard, published by Raphael Tuck & Sons.

'Cheer Up! Things Are Not So Black As They Look'. This design was also used to decorate ceramics with a different caption. Dudley Buxton, J Beagles & Co.

'A GIRL IN EVERY PORT'
TO GREET YOU!

This card is subtitled 'England (Scotland) Home & Beauty'. Fred Spurgin, published by Art and Humour.

THE SILENT PRESSURE
OF THE NAVY.

The allure of the men of the Royal Navy is evident here, as a sailor from an imagined ship called HMS *Teaser* has successfully applied the 'silent pressure'. Jacobus (active 1910s), published by the City Postcard Co.

6

WAR IN THE AIR

The real or imagined threat from Zeppelins dominated the aeronautical comic-card designs of the Great War. By comparison, those of aeroplanes are much harder to find and perhaps this can be explained in part by the technological limitations of planes in the early years of the war and, although they played a prominent part in scouting and reconnaissance missions on the Western Front, most of them did not fly long distances. German floatplane sorties in December 1914 to bomb Britain's coastal towns, including Dover, met with only limited success. However, as the technology developed, the German biplanes – the Gotha and Staaken 'Giant' R-planes – would achieve greater numbers of deaths and destruction of property in 1917 and 1918, far more in fact than all the Zeppelin raids combined. Official estimates list 557 people (including 498 civilians) killed and 1,358 injured, with material damage estimated at £1.5 million (1914–1918 value). The Gotha and 'Giant' raids resulted in 837 deaths and 1,991 injuries, with material damage estimated at a similar level.

What attracted the comic artists to the Zeppelin throughout the war was both its awesome physical appearance and psychological presence. In fact, even before war started its threat was felt through exaggerated factual and fictional accounts of its capabilities in newspapers and magazines. Many of the comic cards focused on people's reactions to the Zeppelin, comparable in size to two football pitches, although the craft itself often didn't feature in the design.

The Zeppelin was an ingenious German invention. Count Ferdinand von Zeppelin (1838–1917) had long realised that the concept of non-rigid airships (ie those without any framework to maintain the shape of the gas bag) was extremely limited, so turned his attention to the design of a rigid vessel. This would have a structural skeleton over which the outer cover would be fitted and in which the hydrogen gas for lifting the airship would be held in a series of gas bags or ballonets to the inside of the frame. It had the advantage that these could be filled and emptied individually and that leaks or punctures in one cell would not lead to the loss of the craft. The Count also calculated that, coupled with a suitable engine, a rigid frame would allow for greater size and lifting power and, on 2 July 1900, the first Zeppelin, LZ 1 (Luftschiff Zeppelin 1), made its first flight over Lake Constance. After a string of successes, failures and setbacks, the Zeppelin, together with the airships produced by rival manufacturer Schütte-Lanz, would ensure that the Zeppelin would become an established part of Germany's army and naval services.

At the outbreak of World War I, Germany possessed just 11 airships, but early offensive operations by army airships over the Eastern and Western Fronts revealed that they were extremely vulnerable to ground fire unless flown at high altitude, and several were lost. London initially had only rudimentary defences and anti-aircraft guns lacked the necessary elevation or range. There was also a lack of trained personnel. In January 1915, following pressure from his advisors, the Kaiser approved the aerial bombardment of Britain, but London was excluded. On 19 January the first raid was carried out by two Zeppelins of the Naval Airship Division, with bombs being dropped on Great Yarmouth and King's Lynn in Norfolk and surrounding villages, killing four people. The long-awaited Zeppelin menace had arrived.

By the end of 1915, there had been 20 raids on Britain, covering an area stretching from Northumberland in the north-east to Kent in the south-east of England, leaving over 200 dead and 500 injured, including the casualties from the first five raids on London between May and October.

The raid of 8–9 September 1915 on central London by Kapitanleutnant Heinrich Mathy, the most successful of all airship commanders, was, in material terms, the most destructive raid of the entire war.

German successes resulted in increasing calls for an effective defence to be put in place to protect London and other counties, since existing anti-aircraft (AA) guns and aircraft had been unable to challenge the Zeppelin's superiority. Measures such as improved AA guns, linked searchlight stations and coordinated aircraft squadrons began to challenge the raiders in early 1916 and, on 1 April, a Zeppelin was brought down by AA fire in the sea north of Margate in Kent.

On 2–3 September 1916, the Germans mounted their largest raid of the war, with 12 airships from the navy and four from the army. The task force was scattered by storms, but a Schütt-Lanz-type, SL-11, an army airship on its first mission, pressed on to London. This prompted a heroic response from 21-year-old Lieutenant William Leefe Robinson of 39 Squadron, Royal Flying Corps. Flying a BE2c biplane, he closed in firing three drums of a new form of ammunition upwards into the airship, which caught fire and fell in a roaring mass of flame, striking the ground at Cuffley in Hertfordshire. The entire crew of 16 died as millions of Londoners cheered the unknown hero who had been the first to shoot down an airship over mainland Britain.

Over the next two days, 10,000 people travelled to the tiny village north of London and police and troops were called in to control the crowds. For shooting down the SL11, Robinson was now the most famous pilot in the country and on 9 September 1916, King George V handed him the Victoria Cross at Windsor Castle. It is now part of the Lord Ashcroft Medal Collection displayed at the Imperial War Museum in London.

After Robinson's success, the Home Defence squadrons seemed to be inspired. On 23 September, 11 airships, including three new 'super' Zeppelins, set out on a raid. L32 was shot down near Great Burstead, near Billericay, Essex by Second Lieutenant Frederick Sowrey, another 39 Squadron pilot. L33 was also brought down at Little Wigborough in Essex and its crew was captured. On the night of 1 October, Heinrich Mathy led another large raid on board L31, but his airship was attacked by Second Lieutenant Wulstan Tempest (also of 39 Squadron) and went down in flames, piling up on the outskirts of Potters Bar, also in Hertfordshire. These German losses proved to be a turning point and Zeppelins no longer attempted to

The alluring spider beckons to the 'flyer', but he points to the sky indicating where his duties lie. William Henry Ellam (1891–1959), published by Geo Pulman & Sons, London.

THE SPIDER AND THE FLY-ER.

attack London; instead, the Germans turned their attention to the industrial areas in the north.

While there were further sporadic raids in 1917 and 1918, the air-raid initiative would now pass from airships to aeroplanes, although the airships had accomplished one of their wartime objectives: to disrupt wartime production. This was because during a threatened raid, factories were forced to black out and stop work. Air-raid precautions meant that thousands of men manned the anti-aircraft guns and searchlights, observers dotted the countryside and trained squadrons had to be allocated to Home Defence duties, all of which diverted vital resources that might otherwise have been deployed on the Western Front.

Comic postcards frequently reflected all of this, featuring black-outs, people and their pets sheltering in some unlikely places, as well as children trying to catch bombs or firing catapults at the airborne menace. The dominant theme of the morale-boosting cards was one of collective resolve, reinforcing the official government message that Britons everywhere could cope with and eventually conquer the Zeppelin threat.

By contrast, depictions of German aeroplanes in comic cards are harder to find. The physical and psychological impact of the Gotha and Giant raids was greater than that caused by the Zeppelins, particularly because many of the initial attacks by Gotha bombers were carried out in broad daylight. The first of these raids on the capital occurred on 13 June 1917, causing 162 deaths and 432 injuries. Among the dead were 16 children, killed by a bomb falling on the Upper North Street primary school in Poplar. This was the deadliest air raid of the war.

Following the switch to night bombing, the 'Harvest Moon' offensive began on 24 September with five raids on London in eight days. Londoners took to the Underground system in increasing numbers for safety and overcrowding became a problem. On 16 February 1918, the first 1,000kg bomb was dropped on the capital by Giant R.39 on the north-east wing of the Royal Hospital Chelsea.

On the few occasions when German planes were depicted in comic cards, they were usually in the distance or shown in an imagined format, sometimes resembling evil-looking birds. Archibald English, who remains a little-known artist, depicts a super-sized policeman with a notice pinned to his chest stating: 'Police Notice Take Cover'. Three boys hide below his vast frame while the devilish-looking German planes, based on the pre-war Taube type, hover ahead, and a third boy runs towards the human shield. The caption reads: 'Come on Billy We're Safe Here'. Another version by the same artist swaps the planes for Zeppelins.

Britain, too, could draw upon a wide range of aeronautical vessels as aircraft became far more sophisticated and differentiated into fighters, bombers and long-range bombers. They were also essential to the conduct of the war since they enabled photo-reconnaissance and artillery observation. Many types of aircraft were made by diverse manufacturers, notably: Airco; Armstrong Whitworth; Avro; Bristol; Martinsyde; Short; Sopwith; Vickers; and Westland. While the development of the rigid airship in Britain lagged far behind the progress made in Germany, Britain successfully used a large number of semi-rigid and non-rigid airships for observation purposes. Together with rigid airships, which became operational later in the war, these were mainly used to counter the U-boat campaign.

A small number of postcard artists tended to glamourise the British airman and their aircraft, imbuing them with an heroic appearance and spirit that persisted well beyond the end of the Great War.

A glamorous lady has been transformed into 'The Raider', a Sopwith Camel. The British biplane appeared on the Western Front in 1917. Kip (active 1910s), published by Raphael Tuck & Sons.

'Looking for Gothas at Manor Park'. A rare card that mentions the Gotha aircraft by name. Artist unknown, published as part of 'The Pioneer Series, London E'.

THE AIR RAIDER

'it 'er 'Arry!

'The Air Raider'. Whether Harry's catapult shot ever reached the Zeppelin is not recorded! George Edward Shepheard, published by Raphael Tuck & Sons.

NEITHER JACK NOR TOMMY CAN
MY WHOLE AFFECTIONS WIN,
BECAUSE I LOVE THE FLYING MAN
WHO BOMBS THE ZEPPELIN.

Following the successes against the Zeppelin in 1916, the brave pilots became well known and this was exploited by government propaganda. Archibald English, published by Wildt & Kray.

The canoodling couple should be leaving immediately! J Forder (active 1910s), published with the reference W 701.

A play on the word 'bomb' which was also short for bombshell, ie a very attractive woman. Artist unknown, published as part of the 'Crown Series No 1112'.

"THERE GOES MY PRIZE MARRER!"

HE: "When we got about a mile high my observer had his leg blown off"

SHE: "How terrible! What an awful wind it must have been"

As Britain developed its own lighter-than-air programme, airships became a much more common sight around the country. Dudley Buxton, published by Inter-Art Co in the 'Twelve-Eighty-Six Series No 1297'.

The quirky Great War humour of Fred Gothard who signed many of his cards with his initials FG is evident here. Published by J Salmon, England No 1477 (Copyright E Mack). This card was not used by post until 25 July 1934 at Blackpool.

IF YOU'VE GOT A NOSE LIKE THIS
DON'T GO OUT AT NIGHT—
OR THE CROWD WILL SHOUT, NOW THE "ZEPPS" ARE ABOUT,
"PUT OUT THAT BLOOMING LIGHT!"

Coming down!

FAR LEFT: Lighting restrictions were rigorously enforced and failure to comply resulted in cases being brought before the courts. Fines were generally around £5. Archibald English, published as part of the 'HB Series No 430'. From a set of six.

LEFT: 'Coming down!' The card celebrates the demise of a Zeppelin in the form of the Kaiser with his famous upturned moustache burning. George Edward Shepheard, published anonymously.

RIGHT: During the early stages of the war people were largely left to their own devices in terms of safety from enemy aircraft, being advised to take to cellars, or to lie down if they were caught in the open. Doug Tempest, published by Bamforth & Co, series no 172.

FAR RIGHT: Sinister black birds are misconstrued as Zeppelins by an old lady who has opened up her umbrella for protection. Doug Tempest, published by Bamforth & Co, series no 294.

'"Here's The Zeppelins, Billy – Come Under Cover!"' Archibald English, published as part of the 'HB Series No 428'.

'"Come on Billy We're safe here."' Sinister-looking German planes have replaced the Zeppelins. Archibald English, published as part of the 'HB Series No 983'.

7

ARMISTICE AND PEACE

Despite the fact that many people believed the war would be over by Christmas 1914, largely because the government encouraged this hope, it took several years of widespread brutal conflict and millions of deaths before hostilities ceased and peace was restored. The fighting on the Western Front ended with the Armistice of 11 November 1918, at 11am Paris time – hence the famous words, 'the eleventh hour of the eleventh day of the eleventh month'. However, further months of discussions and negotiations were required before the Treaty of Versailles was finally signed at the Palace of Versailles, near Paris, on 28 June 1919, thus formally bringing the Great War to a close.

Most of the comic cards relating to peace were produced from November 1918 and ran for several months. In Doug Tempest's design, featured as part of Bamforth & Co's 'Witty Series', a top-hatted winking dove with an olive branch under its wing carries a bag inscribed 'Peace & Co' and is titled 'Keep your pecker up: I'm on the road!'

In a design postally used on 18 November 1918, Dudley Buxton depicts John Bull with a Union Jack waistcoat climbing up the rock face of a mountain without ropes. Below him, red fires and plumes of black smoke billow up with the word 'WAR' overwritten in bold, jagged letters. Bull is almost at the top, where shafts of bright yellow sunshine are inscribed with the words 'Peace and Happiness', although they are not yet as bold as 'WAR'.

Fred Spurgin produced a series of cards to commemorate peace. In one, for the Art and Humour Publishing Co, a drunken man decked with flags of Britain and some of her allies returns to his front door and struggles to find the lock with his key. Above the door handle is a knocker in the form of his disgruntled wife. The headline is 'PEACE' and the caption 'Now for a piece of her mind'.

For the same company, as part of their 'Hopeful' series, Spurgin portrayed a boy and girl observing a partially moonlit night sky inscribed with the word 'PEACE', which is captioned: 'Look on the bright side and peace won't seem so far away'. In another cutesy card from the series the same pair sit hugging astride an anchor, a symbol of hope. It is titled 'There's a Sign of Good Hope. So We're on It!' An example of this card was sent in August 1919, well after the end of war had been formally declared.

A cheery child is decked out in British and allied flags to commemorate the arrival of peace. Fred Spurgin, published by Art and Humour. One of 24 cards.

A dove, the international symbol of hope and peace, clutches under his wing an olive branch and a bag inscribed 'Peace & Co'. Doug Tempest, published by Bamforth & Co.

"Yes, Boys, It's a Hard Climb, BUT WE'LL GET THERE."

After a very hard climb John Bull, the personification of Britain, will reach the summit and thereby restore peace. Dudley Buxton, published by Woolstone Bros, London.

NOW FOR A PIECE OF HER MIND!

'Now For A Piece Of Her Mind'. Note the image of the drunken man's wife on the door knocker. Fred Spurgin, published by Art and Humour.

Pack up your troubles in your old
kit bag and Smile, Smile, 'Smile!—
And while you smile another smiles,
And soon there's miles and miles of smiles;
And life's worth while because you smile,
When you're demobilized!

DEMOBILIZATION

HOME FOR GOOD

A rare card featuring the subject of a soldier being demobbed. Note the sign with the word 'Demobilization' and the kit bag inscribed 'Home For Good'. Doug Tempest, published by Bamforth & Co.

THERE'S A SIGN OF GOOD HOPE, SO WE'RE ON IT!

A sailor and his girlfriend represented by children decked out in red, white and blue (the colours of the Union Jack) sit astride an anchor – a symbol of hope. Fred Spurgin, published by Art and Humour.

BIOGRAPHIES OF THE PRINCIPAL POSTCARD ARTISTS

The information given here about the principal postcard artists who produced comic Great War postcards is largely drawn from an examination of the England & Wales 1911 census returns, supplemented with some additional sources. It reveals fascinating new aspects of the artists' lives, although in comparison with the biographies available on fine artists the details are often sparse.

MABEL LUCIE ATTWELL (1879–1964)

Birthplace: Mile End, East End of London

Education: The Heatherley School of Fine Art and St Martin's School of Art

Additional information: Attwell maintained her maiden name for her work even though she legally changed her surname when she married Harold Earnshaw in 1908. It is known that he sometimes assisted her, in particular with drawing animals and motor vehicles. Attwell worked for various publishers, although her most successful long-term publishing partnership was with Valentine & Sons. She remains the most renowned female postcard artist.

CAPTAIN CHARLES BRUCE BAIRNSFATHER (1887–1959)

Birthplace: Muree, then part of British India, now part of the Punjab province of Pakistan

Education: Westward Ho! School and the John Hassall New School of Art

Additional information: According to the 1911 census, Bairnsfather was at that time living with his parents (his father was a retired Major in the Indian Army) and two servants at Bishopton, Stratford-upon-Avon. Aged 23 and single, his profession is listed as 'Electrical engineer'. However, following time spent serving at the Western Front this would change to artist, in the 1921 census. He is still widely remembered for his trench character 'Old Bill'. Most of his postcards were published by *The Bystander*.

NINA K BRISLEY (1898–1978)

Birthplace: Bexhill, Sussex

Education: Lambeth School of Art

Additional information: Nina Kennard Brisley was one of three artistic daughters born to Constance and George Brisley, the latter of whom worked as a chemist. Of the three sisters, Nina was the standout artist. In addition to illustrational work and designs for postcards, she also produced educational posters. Some of her work was reproduced in *Academy Illustrated*, the magazine of the Royal Academy of Arts, and many of her cards were published by Mansell & Co [Source: Sara Gray, *The Dictionary of Women Artists* (2009)].

ARTHUR BUTCHER (1889–unknown)

Birthplace: Streatham, London

Education: Unknown

Additional information: The 1911 census lists an Arthur Butcher as living at 188, Wellfield Road, Streatham in south London. At that time he was aged 22, single, and his personal occupation was given as 'Business Arts, Apprentice' so it is possible that this was the postcard artist. Butcher was part of a circle of artists that included William Henry Barribal (1874–1952) and Winifred Wimbush (1884–1958), who painted exquisite fashionable women during the 1910s. In his postcards, Butcher enjoyed positioning some of his alluring and sultry ladies in close proximity to officers of His Majesty's forces. His cards were published by Inter-Art Co and Thridgould.

DUDLEY BUXTON (1885–unknown)

Birthplace: Tufnell Park, London

Education: Unknown

Additional information: The 1911 census records Buxton, aged 26, as living at Gordon Avenue, Bognor in Sussex with his wife, mother and sister. His occupation is listed as freelance 'Artist' working at home. Other sources give his birthdate as 1884. Buxton's first passion was the cinema, followed by magazine illustration and especially comic postcards, and he contributed humorous illustrations to *Tatler*. Some of his morale-boosting wartime cards featured on ceramic vases, such as the one that depicts a sailor covered in soot with HMS *Vixen* inscribed on his cap tally and is captioned 'Keep Smiling'. This card was also published with an alternative title: 'Cheer Up! Things Are Not So Black As They Look'. Buxton designed cards for both Beagles and Inter-Art Co. See: www.mckechnies.net/family/buxton/dudley/

REG CARTER (1886–1949)

Birthplace: Southwold, Suffolk

Education: Left Southwold Elementary School at 14 to work for a bricklayer

Additional information: Reginald Arthur Lay Carter turned away from a clerical career in a legal firm to create comic characters for comic strips and magazines. The 1911 census records Carter, aged 24 and single, as living with his parents and elder brother in Bury St Edmunds in Suffolk. His profession is listed as freelance 'Artist (Black & White)'. His father, Francis Wilby Carter, is recorded as being a freelance 'Painter' working from home. Carter designed cards for several publishers, including the British Art Company, E Mack and J Salmon.

AR CATTLEY (1886–1965)

Birthplace: Holloway, London

Education: Unknown

Additional information: Alexander Robert Cattley is recorded in the 1911 census as living in Stoke Newington, London with his parents, two brothers and three sisters. He was aged 25, single, and listed as being a freelance 'Black & White Artist'. From Tim Cattley, a descendant of the artist, it is known that he worked for the *News Chronicle* and was an authority on military uniforms. Cattley produced cards for Photochrom Co.

GEO DAVEY (1882–unknown)

Birthplace: Islington, London

Education: Unknown

Additional information: George Davey is listed in the 1911 census as being aged 29 and living with his wife and cousin in Cricklewood in north-west London. He worked as an 'Artist' for 'The Press'. Davey produced work for a wide variety of comics and magazines, including *Punch*. One of his popular creations was 'Dreamy Daniel', a tramp who during his sleep went on adventures. He featured in *Lot-O-Fun* from 1906 to 1922 and proved such a hit with the public that the character and his antics were transformed into a stage performance. Davey designed cards for the James Henderson publishing company.

HAROLD CECIL EARNSHAW (1886–1937)

Birthplace: Woodford, Essex

Education: St Martin's School of Art

Additional information: The 1911 census reveals that Harold Cecil Earnshaw and Mabel Lucie Attwell were living at 'Casita', Fanfare Road, Coulsdon in Surrey. He was 24, Mabel was 31. They had one daughter and were assisted by two servants. His birthdate is recorded on the form as 1887, although other sources indicate a year of 1886. The professions of both Earnshaw and Mabel were noted as freelance 'Painter (Artist)'. He worked for

The Bystander and *Tatler* and produced comic strips for *The Graphic* and *Daily Mirror.* Earnshaw created cards for Millar & Lang Art Publishing Co, Photochrom Co, J Salmon and Valentine & Sons.

ARCHIBALD ENGLISH (1881–unknown)

Birthplace: Lambeth, London
Education: Unknown
Additional information: English is listed in the 1911 census as being aged 30 and single, living at 51, Coldharbour Lane, Camberwell in London with his mother, a widow, and his four sisters. His profession was given as freelance 'Black & White Artist'. He designed cards for the City Postcard Co, Corona, Hutson Bros, Thridgould and Wildt & Kray.

THOMAS COSTERTON GILSON (1885–1971)

Birthplace: Bromley, Kent
Education: Unknown
Additional information: Gilson's father was a fishmonger and his mother a dressmaker. By 1901, the family had relocated to Battersea in London and at that time Gilson was working as a draughtsman for an upholsterer. In 1911, the census reveals that he was active as a black-and-white artist and still resident in Battersea, but now living with his wife, mother and grandfather.

Gilson contributed designs to the Alpha publishing company and the 'Ludgate Series' for EJH & Co.

FRED GOTHARD (1882–1971)

Birthplace: Holmfirth, West Yorkshire
Education: Unknown
Additional information: Fred Gothard successfully balanced a dual life of working in a bank by day and freelancing as a cartoonist whenever he could find the time. The 1911 census reveals that at the age of 29 he was still working as a bank clerk but was boarding in a home in Birkenhead, Merseyside. He either worked close by or perhaps in Liverpool. His cartooning did not detract from his bank work as he ended his career as a bank manager in Manchester. Gothard designed cards for Photochrom Co and J Salmon.

ALFRED LEETE (1882–1933)

Birthplace: Thorpe Achurch, Northamptonshire
Education: Kingsholme School and the School of Science and Art, Weston-super-Mare
Additional information: Alfred Ambrose Chew Leete was listed in the 1911 census as being aged 29 and living with his wife Edith, aged 31, at numbers 2, 4, 6 & 8 St Stephen's Road, Bayswater in London. His profession is given as 'Hotel proprietor'. The regular income from this

business enabled Leete to focus on comic work on a freelance basis without the money worries that plagued many artists. The census also reveals that they had lost their child, probably only a few days after birth. Leete's designs were published by Bamforth & Co, Beagles, Lawrence & Jellicoe and Valentine & Sons.

FREDERICK GEORGE LEWIN (1861–1933)

Birthplace: Bristol
Education: Old Trades School, Bristol
Additional information: Lewin is listed in the 1911 census as being aged 50 and living with his wife and son at 10, Burlington Road, Redland in Bristol. His occupation is given as 'artist'. Lewin turned away from journalism to pursue his ambition of being a freelance commercial artist. He became an associate of the Royal West of England Academy in 1904 and a full member in 1907. We know that the census was filled out by the artist himself as it has the characteristics of his signature featured on his postcards. He produced cards for Inter-Art Co, J Salmon and EW Savory Ltd.

HGC MARSH-LAMBERT (1888–1981)

Birthplace: Bristol
Education: Unknown
Additional information: Helen Grace Culverwell Marsh-Lambert is listed in the 1911 census under her maiden name Marsh. She was aged 23, single and living with her parents and one servant in Barnet, north London. Her profession is given as 'Artist (Book Illustrator)'. These books include: *Mother Goose Rhymes* (1914); *Tiny Toddlers* (1916); *Collin's Playtime ABC* (1919); *Rhymes and Riddles With My Very Own Pictures* (1926); *My Little Nature Book With My Very Own Pictures* (1930); *Favourite Nursery Rhymes* (1939); and *Jack and Jill's Easy Storybook* (1950). Anthony Byatt notes in *Picture Postcards and their Publishers* (1978) that she worked for Davidson Bros and that in 1915 she: 'designed an interesting series entitled *Girls for the Allies* which showed a girl from each country with a large flag in the background. She also drew *Khaki Kiddies* which proved very successful.' Marsh-Lambert also worked for CW Faulkner & Co and Photochrom Co.

FERGUS MACKAIN (1886–1924)

Birthplace: St John, New Brunswick, Canada
Education: Unknown
Additional information: Private Fergus HE Mackain was the second of seven children of a civil engineer who had emigrated from England to North America before the war. Fergus was already settled in New York with his own family when he responded to the call to arms and returned to Europe to fight, after which he returned to New York on

9 September 1920. Reg Mayhew, the artist's third cousin three times removed, notes that on the passenger manifest at Ellis Island in 1920 Mackain was recorded as being: '6ft 3 inches tall with a fresh complexion, fair hair and blue eyes.' His cards in the 'Sketches of Tommy's Life' series were published in France by P Gaultier, Boulogne-sur-Mer and G Savigny, Paris.

DONALD MCGILL (1875–1962)

Birthplace: Marylebone, London
Education: Blackheath Proprietary School
Additional information: Donald Fraser Gould McGill is listed in the 1911 census as living at 48, Malvern Road, Surbiton in Surrey. Aged 36, he was the head of a household that included his wife Florence and two daughters, Mary and Margaret. His occupation is recorded as being 'Artist' working at home. McGill remains *the* brand name for all comic postcards, although his family remained deeply embarrassed about his chosen profession. All of his Great War cards were published by Inter-Art Co.

REG MAURICE (active mid-1910s to 1970s)

Birthplace: Sydney, Australia
Education: Fettes, Edinburgh
Additional information: Initially, it was considered that the artist could possibly be the 'Reg Maurice' listed in the English census record of 1911 who was born in Peckham and by this date was living with his family at 4, Alderbrook Road, Balham in London. However, there is another, more likely, contender: Rollo Paterson (1892–1978). Paterson was born in Australia to parents of Scottish origin, who sent him to study in Edinburgh and Sterling (his father's birthplace). Paterson remained in the UK to pursue a career as a fine artist, supplementing his income during lean periods (of which there were many) with numerous comic-postcard designs under various pseudonyms, including Reg Maurice and Vera Paterson. Many of Reg Maurice's designs were published by the Regent Publishing Co. I am grateful to Bernard Crossley for bringing this to my attention.

FE MORGAN (active 1910s–1930s)

Birthplace: Unknown
Education: Unknown
Additional information: FE Morgan does not seem to appear in the UK census records. It is, however, known that he produced a wide range of cards, including those relating to wartime economy and rationing, for Inter-Art Co, Photochrom Co, George Pulman & Sons, J Salmon and Raphael Tuck & Sons.

AA NASH (1889–unknown)

Birthplace: Kensington, London

Education: Art School in London

Additional information: By the time of the 1911 census Adrienne Nash was 22, single and living with her parents, sister and a servant at 87, Gunterstone Road, West Kensington. Her profession is recorded as 'Art Student', so this may well be the same person as the postcard artist. Samuel, her father, was considerably older than her at 63 and worked as a fur dealer. She designed cards for Inter-Art Co.

ERNEST NOBLE (1882–unknown)

Birthplace: Stoke Newington, London

Education: Unknown

Additional information: Ernest Noble was the son of a Quaker minister. The 1911 census records him as living with his parents and sister with one servant at 33, Ashfield Avenue, Kings Heath, a suburb of Birmingham. Noble was aged 29 and listed as being married, although his wife's name is not included. His profession is given as 'newspaper artist'. Many of his cards are identified not by a publisher but by a three-figure number followed by the words 'British Manufacture'.

GEO PIPER (1887–unknown)

Birthplace: Beccles, Suffolk

Education: Unknown

Additional information: George Henry Herbert Piper is listed in the 1911 census as being aged 24, single and living with his parents, sister and a lodger at 50, Deacon Road, Kingston-upon-Thames, Surrey. His occupation is recorded as 'artist (designer)'. Piper produced some cards for the City Postcard Co and E Mack.

SID A POTTS (1886–unknown)

Birthplace: Ponders End, Middlesex

Education: Unknown

Additional information: By 1911, Sidney Atkinson Potts was aged 25. He had been married for less than a year and he was listed as being a freelance artist working in black-and-white and colour for the newspapers. He lived at 71, Myddleton Square in the City of London. Potts designed cards for Gale & Polden.

AGNES RICHARDSON (1885–1951)

Birthplace: Wimbledon, Surrey

Education: Lambeth School of Arts

Additional information: The 1911 census lists Agnes Richardson, aged 26 and single, as living with her two sisters at 6, Bernard Gardens, Wimbledon. Her personal occupation is recorded as 'Designer'. She is featured in the *Dictionary of Women Artists* (2009) as Kate Agnes Richardson (although she didn't use her Christian name), the youngest of eight children whose mother died when she was only six. She was helped by her brother, Robert, who was an enthusiastic painter and won some art competitions. After art school she worked in a printer's studio, which helped to launch a prolific career that lasted for more than 40 years, during which she designed posters for the London Underground Group across the years 1912–1922. Richardson designed cards for Inter-Art Co, E Mack, Photochrom Co and Raphael Tuck & Sons.

WILLIAM STOCKER SHAW (1879/80–1945)

Birthplace: London
Education: Unknown
Additional information: William Stocker Shaw's marriage certificate of 22 August 1908 records him as being aged 28, the son of a watchmaker and working as an artist. His address is given as 360, Uxbridge Road, Shepherd's Bush in London. For such a prolific and versatile postcard practitioner, frustratingly little is known of this artist. He worked for various publishers including the City Postcard Co, Davidson Bros, Thridgould and Woolstone Bros. Shaw's drawing style

appears a little naive, although charming, and not as assured as that of, for instance, Donald McGill or Fred Spurgin. However, his passionate commitment to the genre of comic cards cannot be doubted.

GE SHEPHEARD [GES] (1869–unknown)

Birthplace: North Walsham, Norfolk
Education: Unknown
Additional information: George Edward Shepheard is listed in the 1911 census as being aged 42, married and with one son, living at 93, Lauderdale Mansions, Maida Vale, Paddington in London. Shepheard's profession was recorded as freelance 'artist (Painter)' working from home. He produced cards for the Avenue Publishing Co, Faulkner and Raphael Tuck & Sons and collaborated with George Alexander Stevens [GAS] on a series of quirky black-and-white silhouette designs depicting army camp life for Photochrom Co.

FRED SPURGIN (1885–1966)

Birthplace: Russia
Education: Unknown
Additional information: Frederick Spurgin is listed in the 1911 census as being aged 26, single and living in 20, Wiltshire Road, Brixton in London with his father, who worked as a watch- and jewellery-repairer, along

with three brothers, one sister and a servant. The professions of Fred and his brother Maurice, then aged 20, are both recorded as 'Artist & Designer'. If Spurgin's father Solomon had been in the furniture business in Birmingham, as Brian Lund has suggested, there is no evidence that this continued once they had relocated to London. Among the books Spurgin illustrated are: *Pat, Peggy and the Pub* (1910); *Cinderella* (1915); *Jours Heureux* (1920); *A Toyland Story* (1920); and *Pat and Peggy in Cave-Land* (1932). His cards were published by several companies, notably the Art and Humour Publishing Co, Inter-Art Co and Thridgould.

VW STERNBERG [VWS] (active 1910s–1930s)

Birthplace: Unknown
Education: Unknown
Additional information: VW Sternberg is perhaps the same artist who signed cards with the initials 'V. W. S.'. However, the style of work varies from being masculine to feminine, so it is also possible that they are different people. AW Coysh in his *The Dictionary of Picture Postcards in Britain 1894–1939* (1984) believes it is one and the same man and notes that his cards were published by James Henderson & Sons Ltd, the Regent Publishing Co and Valentine & Sons.

GEORGE ALEXANDER STEVENS [GAS]

(1882–unknown)
Birthplace: London
Education: Unknown
Additional information: In 1911, Stevens is listed in the census records as being aged 29 and living with his father, mother, sister and one servant at 18, Grange Road, Gunnersbury, Chiswick in what is now west London. His profession is recorded as freelance artist. Edwin William Stevens, his father, was also working as an employed 'lithographic artist'. George Alexander Stevens (GAS) collaborated with GE Shepheard (GES) on a series of black-and-white silhouette designs of army camp life and another on wartime economy and rationing for Photochrom Co.

GEORGE E STUDDY (1878/9–1948)

Birthplace: Stoke Damerel, Devon
Education: Clifton College, Bristol; Dulwich College; The Heatherley School of Fine Art; and Calderon's School of Animal Painting.
Additional information: Although already an established artist by 1911, George Ernest Studdy is listed in the census as being one of three boarders living in the home of Mary Breman, a widow. He was 32, single, and working as an 'artist'. While a student he met Harold

Earnshaw and Mabel Lucie Attwell at The Heatherley School of Fine Art. Although he produced various subjects – notably some charming depictions of children – it was his Bonzo canine creation that was most in demand. Cuppleditch reports that Studdy used to say: '"I could have made a fortune out of Bonzo"; instead he chose the peaceful cloistered life of a lonely bachelor with his dogs and gentlemen's club.' In fact, he did marry, but the relationship was short-lived. Studdy contributed Great War designs to Mansell and Valentine & Sons. From the 1920s, his Bonzo cards were published by Inter-Art Co.

DOUG TEMPEST (1887–1954)

Birthplace: Thurlton, Norfolk

Education: Leeds School of Art

Additional information: Oddly, the census records do not list this artist under Douglas or Doug Tempest. It is known from other sources that he was living at 8, Whardale Street in Leeds, West Yorkshire from 1901 until 1937, when records show that he moved to Holmfirth, where his employer, Bamforth & Co, had its headquarters. Tempest joined the company in the 1910s and was still working there in the 1950s. Tempest's anti-Kaiser cards derived from the series of 48 magic lantern slides he produced for Bamforth & Co in 1914.

BERT THOMAS (1883–1966)

Birthplace: Newport, Monmouthshire

Education: Apprenticed to an engraver in Swansea

Additional information: Herbert Samuel Thomas was popularly known as Bert. He is recorded in the 1911 census as being aged 27, living with his wife, a nurse, at St Stephen's Crescent, Paddington in London. His profession was described as a freelance 'Black & White artist' and he worked at home. His cards were published by Gale & Polden and Raphael Tuck & Sons.

LOUIS WAIN (1860–1939)

Birthplace: Clerkenwell, London

Education: West London School of Art

Additional information: Wain is listed in the 1911 census as being aged 49, a widower, living with four sisters and a servant at 'Bendigo', Collingwood Terrace, Westgate-on-Sea, Kent. His occupation is given as freelance 'Artist (Painter)' working at home. His birth year is recorded as 1862 here, which differs from the 1860 date indicated by most other records. Wain and his family moved back to London in 1917. He was the most committed artist to one particular subject, cats, and his anthropomorphic feline friends – often featured with large eyes – were enlisted to support the war effort. Wain suffered long periods of poor health and died penniless, although his postcards are among the most sought-after today. He painted cats covered in the Union Jack flag marching, holding artillery shells, in the trenches on the Western Front, and recovering from their battle wounds back in Britain. Occasionally, he painted dogs. His cards were published by various companies, including Davidson Bros, CW Faulkner & Co, Raphael Tuck & Sons and Valentine & Sons.

FLORA WHITE (1878–1953)

Birthplace: Brighton
Education: Brighton School of Art
Additional information: White was the daughter of a Jabez White, a wood-carver, and Adele Naldini, an Italian housewife, who named Flora and her four sisters after Greek goddesses. By 1915, three key events had occurred: her father had died, her mother had remarried and the family business had been broken up. White then focused on a career as a commercial artist and illustrator of children's books. Her wartime cards were published by Hutson Bros, E Mack, Photochrom Co and J Salmon. [source: Sara Gray, *The Dictionary of Women Artists* (2009).]

LAWSON WOOD (1878–1957)

Birthplace: Highgate, London
Education: The Slade School of Fine Art, The Heatherley School of Fine Art and Calderon's School of Animal Painting
Additional information: By 1911, Clarence Lawson Wood was listed in the census as being aged 32 and married with two sons, one daughter and two servants, living in Albert Road, Bexhill-on-Sea in East Sussex. His birth date is given here as being 1879, whereas other sources indicate it was 1878. Wood's occupation was recorded as freelance 'Artist (Picture Painter & Illustrator)'. His cards were published by many companies, including Carlton Publishing Co; Davidson Bros; Dobson, Molle & Co; Inter-Art Co; Lawrence & Jellicoe; J Salmon; Raphael Tuck & Sons; and Valentine & Sons.

BIBLIOGRAPHY

Alderson Frederick, *The Comic Postcard in English Life*, David & Charles, 1970

Attwell, Mabel Lucie, interview in *The Strand Magazine*, no 552, December 1936

Baile de Laperriere, Charles (ed), *The Society of Women Artists Exhibitors, 1855–1996*, Hilmarton Manor Press, 1996

Barrett, Michèle and Stallybrass, Peter, 'Printing, Writing and a Family Archive: Recording the First World War', *History Workshop Journal*, Issue 75, 2013

Batchelor, Tim, Lewisohn, Cedar and Myrone, Martin (eds), *Rude Britannia: British Comic Art*, Tate Publishing, 2010

Beetles, Chris, *Mabel Lucie Attwell*, Chris Beetles Ltd, 1997

Braithwaite, Paul, 'Free Photochrom Handbook', *Picture Postcard Monthly*, no 436, August 2015

Bryant, Mark, 'Charles Bruce Bairnsfather, 1887–1959', *Oxford Dictionary of National Biography*, Oxford University Press, 2004

Byatt, Anthony, *Picture Postcards and their Publishers*, Golden Age Postcard Books, 1978

Buckland, Alfred, *The World of Donald McGill*, Blandford, 1984

Calder-Marshall, Arthur, *Wish You Were Here: The Art of Donald McGill*, Hutchinson, 1966

Carline, Richard, *Pictures in the Post: The Story of the Picture Postcard and its Place in the History of Popular Art*, Gordon Fraser Gallery Ltd, 1971

Clark, Alan, *Dictionary of British Comic Artists, Writers and Editors*, The British Library, 1998

Cox, Howard and Mowatt, Simon, *Revolutions from Grub Street: A History of Magazine Publishing in Britain*, Oxford University Press, 2014

Cox, Michael, *Women at War on Old Picture Postcards*, Brian Lund, 2014

Coysh, AW, *The Dictionary of Picture Postcards in Britain 1894–1939*, Antique Collectors' Club, 1984

Crossley, Bernard, *Donald McGill – Postcard Artist*, Greaves & Thomas, 2014

Crossley, Bernard, 'Donald McGill – The One and Only: A Brief Introduction to the "Master" and His Work', *Picture Postcard Monthly*, no 442, February 2016

Crossley, Bernard, 'The World War I Postcards of Donald McGill', *Picture Postcard Monthly*, no 424, August 2014

Cuppleditch, David, *The London Sketch Club*, Alan Sutton Publishing Ltd, 1994

Donnelley, Paul, 'Rarely seen postcards show Britain's king of the saucy seaside humour McGill turned his hand to the First World War effort', *Mail Online*, 25 July 2014

Doyle, Peter, *British Postcards of the First World War*, Shire Library, 2011

Doyle, Peter, *The British Soldier of the First World War*, Shire Library, 2014

Dunn, Julian, 'Stepping on the GAS' [GA Stevens], *Picture Postcard Monthly*, no 335, March 2007

Gosling, Lucinda, *A Better 'Ole: The Brilliant Bruce Bairnsfather and the First World War*, The History Press, 2014

Gosling, Lucinda, *Brushes & Bayonets: Cartoons, Sketches and Paintings of World War I*, Osprey, 2008

Gray, Sara, *The Dictionary of Women Artists*, The Lutterworth Press, 2009

Hanna, Martha, 'War Letters: Communication between Front and Home Front', *International Encyclopaedia of the First World War* [online], October 2014

Hardy, Rev EJ, *The British Soldier: His Courage and Humour*, T Fisher Unwin, 1915

Hauskeller, Michael, 'Felix, Mickey Mouse, and the Comic Genius of Dudley Buxton', *Picture Postcard Monthly*, no 374, June 2010

Henty, John, *The Collectable World of Mabel Lucie Attwell*, Richard Dennis, 1999

Holt, Tonie and Valmai, *In Search of the Better 'Ole: The Biography of Captain Bruce Bairnsfather*, Leo Cooper, 2001

Holt, Tonie and Valmai, *Till the Boys Come Home: The Picture Postcards of the First World War*, Macdonald and Jane's, 1977, revised and reprinted by Pen & Sword Military, 2014

Horne, Alan, *Dictionary of 20th Century British Book Illustrators*, Antique Collectors' Club, 1994

Houfe, Simon, *Dictionary of British Book Illustrators and Caricaturists 1800–1914*, Antique Collectors' Club, 1978

Huckstep, Hilary, 'In tribute of Reg Carter', *Picture Postcard Monthly*, no 434, June 2015

Huckstep, Hilary, 'Pursuing Reg' [Reg Carter], *Picture Postcard Monthly*, no 381, January 2011

Huckstep, Hilary, 'Reg Carter remembered', *Picture Postcard Monthly*, no 302, June 2004

Kearns, Seamus, 'Collecting Picture Postcards', *Dublin Historical Record*, Vol 54, No 2, 2001

Kennedy, Alistair, 'Postal history from British forces on the Western Front in 1914', *Stamp Magazine*, August 2014

Klich, Lynda and Weiss, Benjamin, *The Postcard Age*, Thames & Hudson, 2012

Laffin, John, *World War I in Postcards*, 1988 and reprinted by Wrens Park in 2001

Lewis, Brian, 'Will the real FS [Fred Spurgin] please stand up!', *Picture Postcard Monthly*, no 359, March 2009

Lund, Brian, 'Bonzo, "The mischievous Postcard Pup"', *Picture Postcard Monthly*, no 322, February 2006

Lund, Brian, 'Checklist of Inter-Art postcards by Fred Spurgin', *Picture Postcard Monthly*, no 84, April 1986

Lund, Brian, 'Checklist of Inter-Art postcards by Fred Spurgin' [continued], *Picture Postcard Monthly*, no 85, May 1986

Lund, Brian, 'Fred Spurgin's Inter-Art postcards' [an addendum to the checklist in April/May 1998, PPM], *Picture Postcard Monthly*, no 87, July 1986

Lund, Brian, *Joining Up: Oh We Don't Want to Lose You (on old picture postcards)*, Reflections of a Bygone Age, 2014

Lund, Brian, *Patriotism: My Country Right or Wrong (on old picture postcards)*, Reflections of a Bygone Age, 2014

Lund, Brian, *Propaganda in the First World War (on old picture postcards)*, Reflections of a Bygone Age, 2014

Lund, Brian, 'The Postcards of AA Nash' [a checklist of the artist's work], *Picture Postcard Monthly*, no 87, July 1986

Lund, Brian, 'The versatile Fred Spurgin', *Picture Postcard Monthly*, no 84, April 1986

McDonald, Ian, 'The Screw Tightens' [rationing and restrictions in World War I], *Picture Postcard Monthly*, no 87, July 1986

Ministry of Information (various authors), 'The Organisation and Functions of the Ministry of Information' and reports of

The War Propaganda Bureau. Contained in the same file, The National Archives, Kew; Reference: INF 4/5

Noakes, FE, *The Distant Drum: A Memoir of a Guardsman in the Great War*, Frontline Books, 2010

Orwell, George, 'The Art of Donald McGill', *Horizon – A Review of Literature and Art*, September 1941

Osborn, Tony, 'Any more FG Lewin fans out there?', *Picture Postcard Monthly*, no 132, April 1990 [see also PPM, March 1988]

Osborn, Tony, 'Comic talent with a wide repertoire: the under-rated postcards skills of FG Lewin', *Picture Postcard Monthly*, no 215, March 1997

Richards, Anthony, 'Letter censorship on the front line', *The Telegraph* online, 30 May 2014

Saunders, ML, 'Wellington House and British Propaganda during the First World War', *The Historical Journal*, Vol 18, no 1, March 1975

Scott, Peter T, *Home For Christmas: Cards, Messages and Legends of the Great War*, Tom Donovan Publishing Ltd, 1993

Skeef, Ralph, 'Lots more GAS' [GA Stevens], *Picture Postcard Monthly,* no 336, April 2007

Skeef, Ralph, 'Even more GAS' [GA Stevens], *Picture Postcard Monthly,* no 340, August 2007

Storey, Neil R and Housego, Molly, *Women in the First World War*, Shire Library, 2010

Suggitt, Stan, 'The Derby Armlet', *Picture Postcard Monthly*, no 191, March 1995

2 PACK UP YOUR TROUBLES

Taylor, James, *Careless Talk Costs Lives: Fougasse & the Art of Public Information*, Conway, 2010

Taylor, James, *Your Country Needs You: The Secret History of the Propaganda Poster*, Saraband, 2013

Thatcher, Martyn and Quinn, Anthony, *The Amazing Story of the Kitchener Poster*, Funfly Design, 2013

Thomas, Vikki (ed), *Mabel Keeps Calm and Carries On: The Wartime Postcards of Mabel Lucie Attwell*, The History Press, 2013

Tholas-Disset, C and Ritzenhoff, K (eds), *Humor, Entertainment, and Popular Culture during World War I*, Palgrave Macmillian US, 2015

Tucker, Peter, 'Douglas Tempest's protection racket', *Picture Postcard Monthly*, no 217, May 1997

Tucker, Peter, 'The Comic Cards of Donald McGill and Douglas Tempest in World War I', *Picture Postcard Annual*, 1996 edition

Wollaeger, Mark, *Modernism, Media, and Propaganda: British Narrative from 1900 to 1945*, Princeton University Press, 2008

Williams, David M, 'A New Medium for Advertising: the Postcard, 1900–1920', *European Journal of Marketing*, Vol 22, Issue 8, 1988

Willoughby, Martin, *A History of Postcards*, Bracken Books, 1994

Wood, Jeremy, *Hidden Talents: A Dictionary of Neglected Artists Working 1880–1950*, Jeremy Wood Fine Art, 1994

COPYRIGHT OF WORLD WAR I POSTCARDS

In most cases the postcard artists assigned the copyright of their designs to the publisher, of which there were many in the Great War period. Almost all of these publishing companies have long since ceased trading, the original printing plates have been destroyed, lost or recycled, and their assets have been liquidated, leaving no clear indication of who holds the copyright. Reasonable reproduction fees will be paid to the copyright holder(s) on the provision of proof of a contract valid under UK law in 2016. Please send details to: YCNYPostcard@aol.com.

INDEX